StayMarried: A Couples Devotional

A SIMPLE WEEKLY GUIDE TO DEEPEN YOUR CONNECTION, STRENGTHEN YOUR FAITH, AND BUILD A LASTING, JOYFUL MARRIAGE

EMMETT KRISCE | EMELINE KRISCE

GRAPEVINE BOOKS

Published by

GRAPEVINE BOOKS

www.grapevinebooks.com

email: contact@grapevinebooks.com

Ordering Information:

Quantity sales: Special discounts are available on quantity purchases by corporations, associations, and others.

For details, reach out to the publisher.

First published by Grapevine Books, 2025

CONTENTS

1. Three Strands

"Though one may be overpowered, two can defend themselves.
A cord of three strands is not quickly broken."
Ecclesiastes 4:12

The rain had been steady all afternoon, tapping softly against the kitchen windows as Daniel and Lily cleaned up after dinner. Their teenage daughter had drifted upstairs to finish homework, and their son was sprawled across the living room floor, building an elaborate tower of wooden blocks. Daniel reached for a dish towel while Lily rinsed the plates, and for a moment the only sound was the hum of the dishwasher and the rhythmic patter of rain.

It had been a long week. Work deadlines, unexpected bills, and a few tense conversations had left both of them feeling worn thin. But now, here in the quiet glow of their home, something felt different. Daniel noticed Lily pause, her hands resting on the edge of the sink. She looked tired, but her eyes softened when he stepped closer. He placed a hand on her shoulder, and she leaned into the touch, letting out a breath she had been holding all day.

They did not say much, but they did not need to. In that quiet moment they remembered what they often forgot in the rush of life. They were not standing alone. God had woven their lives together, strand by strand, and His presence was still holding them steady.

***

Ecclesiastes teaches many truths about the seasons of life, and in this verse the writer gives a simple but beautiful picture of strength. He says that a single strand can snap easily. Two strands are stronger, yet still vulnerable. But three strands twisted together form a cord that holds under pressure. This image would have been familiar to people in ancient times, since ropes were made by weaving fibers tightly until they were firm and dependable.

In marriage, the Lord invites us to see ourselves in this picture. A husband alone can grow weary. A wife alone can feel overwhelmed. Even together, two people can find themselves stretched thin by stress, temptation, or exhaustion. But when God is the third strand, something changes. His presence binds the couple together with a strength they cannot create on their own. He becomes the steady center that keeps them from unraveling when life feels heavy.

This does not mean a marriage will be free from difficulty. It means God gives stability where our human efforts fall short. He is the one who helps couples stay patient, forgiving, gentle, and faithful. When a husband and wife walk with Him daily, their union takes on a strength that endures.

The idea of a threefold cord reminds us that marriage is not simply a partnership between two individuals. It is a sacred union that God Himself designed to reflect His wisdom and kindness. When the writer of Ecclesiastes speaks of this woven strength, he is pointing to something deeper than physical structure. He is pointing to the spiritual truth that our relationships were never meant to survive on human strength alone.

We live in a world that often encourages independence above all else. Many couples start out believing they can handle anything on their own. They trust their compatibility, or their shared goals, or their good intentions. Those things matter, but they cannot supply the lasting strength a lifelong covenant requires. Sooner or later, every marriage meets challenges that stretch it beyond natural ability. Stress builds. Emotions flare. Disappointments surface. Life brings unexpected storms, and what once felt effortless becomes demanding.

This passage offers hope for those moments. It reminds us that God is not distant from our daily struggles. He is present in the tired mornings, the busy evenings, and the long conversations that shape a household. When couples invite Him into their marriage, they discover a strength that grows quietly and steadily, like a tree taking root in good soil.

A cord woven with three strands is not formed in a moment. It is created by twisting one strand around another again and again. In the same way, a marriage strengthened by God is shaped through daily habits that draw both spouses toward Him. Simple choices make a difference. Praying together, even briefly, helps bind hearts with humility and trust. Reading Scripture together brings clarity and peace. Attending church as a family reminds each person that they belong to something bigger than themselves. Acts of kindness and forgiveness become threads God uses to reinforce unity.

When the Lord becomes the third strand, He also brings healing where there has been strain. He softens harsh words, restores emotional closeness, and steadies a couple when fear or worry threatens to divide them. Some couples carry old wounds or memories that feel heavy. Others struggle with the pressure of raising children, managing finances, or balancing work. God does not ignore these burdens. He stands ready to strengthen the areas of marriage that feel fragile.

There is beauty in remembering that two people, no matter how different, can be held together by the loving hands of God. He does not force unity, but He invites it. He invites husbands and wives to lean on Him when they feel tired, to trust Him when they feel uncertain, and to let Him renew their bond when life grows complicated.

A cord of three strands is not easily broken because the strength does not come from the strands alone. It comes from the way they are woven together. In the same way, a marriage rooted in God's presence gains a resilience that lasts through every season.

FROM HIS PERSPECTIVE

When I first heard this verse as a young man, I understood it in theory but not in experience. Now, after years of marriage, its truth sits deeply in my heart. I have seen how quickly my patience can fade on hard days. I have felt the weight of responsibility and the pressure to hold everything together. There have been moments when I leaned too much on my own strength and ended up frustrated or discouraged.

But then I remember that God never asked me to carry the load alone. When I choose to bring Him into my decisions, my words, and my marriage, something shifts. I grow calmer. I listen better. I love with more steadiness. I realize that my wife and I are not two people holding on by ourselves. We are part of a cord God Himself is strengthening. Knowing that gives me peace, even in the busiest seasons.

FROM HER PERSPECTIVE

This passage reminds me of the quiet ways God has held our marriage over the years. I have watched myself become anxious, tired, or overly sensitive in certain seasons, and I have seen how easily fear can creep into my thoughts. Yet every time I turn my heart back to the Lord, I feel a gentle steadiness rise within me. He softens my tone when I want to snap. He helps me see my husband with tenderness instead of frustration. He gives me patience I did not have on my own.

There is comfort in knowing God truly cares about the daily rhythms of our relationship. He is present when we disagree, when we laugh, and when we simply go about the routines of family life. When I remember that He is the third strand in our cord, I feel secure. I feel hopeful. And I feel grateful for the strength He brings.

PRAYER

Lord, thank You for weaving our lives together with Your steady hands. Strengthen our marriage with Your peace, guide our words with gentleness, and help us lean on You in every season. Make us aware of Your presence in our home and teach us to trust You in both small and great moments. Bind our hearts together with Your love and keep our marriage rooted in You. Amen.

CONVERSATION PROMPTS

1. When do you feel the strongest sense of emotional closeness between us, and what small choices or habits help create that feeling for you? How can we become more intentional this week about protecting those moments and nurturing a deeper connection in our daily rhythm together?

2. What is something in our marriage that you feel God has strengthened recently, and what is one area where you feel we need His help or guidance? How can we support each other in that area with kindness, patience, and consistent prayer throughout the week?

CONNECTION PRACTICES

Tonight, hold hands and pray a simple prayer asking God to strengthen your bond and guide the week ahead. After praying, each of you choose one intentional act of kindness to bless the other before the day ends. It can be small, quiet, or practical, but offered with genuine care. Later, talk briefly about how these two choices made you feel and whether they helped you feel closer, calmer, or more connected.

2. Choosing Love Daily

"And above all these things put on charity,
which is the bond of perfectness."
Colossians 3:14

In 1990, Robertson McQuilkin, then the respected president of Columbia Bible College, made a decision that caught national attention. His wife, Muriel, had been slowly losing her memory to Alzheimer's, and caring for her was becoming more demanding every year. She no longer recognized many friends. She often grew anxious when he was away. Yet Robertson noticed something remarkable. Even as her mind faded, Muriel remained calm whenever he was near. Her face brightened when he walked into the room, and she clung to him with a childlike trust.

After much prayer, Robertson announced he would step down from his position. Many urged him to continue leading, offering caregivers and support. But he knew the choice he needed to make. He said his decision was not based on duty alone. It was based on love. He explained that loving Muriel was a daily calling, not a burden, and he wanted to give her the best of himself in her final years.

When he cared for her, she rested more peacefully. When he spoke gently to her, she smiled. The world saw a man giving up status. Robertson saw it as choosing love, one quiet day at a time.

***

Colossians 3:14 tells us to put on love, describing it as the virtue that binds everything together in perfect unity. This verse appears within a passage that encourages believers to clothe themselves with compassion, kindness, humility, gentleness, and patience. These qualities create a healthy community, and Scripture singles out love as the thread that holds all the other virtues in place. Without it, even the best intentions can unravel.

In marriage, this truth becomes especially clear. A husband and wife will have moments of joy, but they will also have times when stress, misunderstanding, or exhaustion make love feel difficult. God knows this, which is why He calls us to "put on" love. It is an action, not just an emotion. It involves choosing to respond with kindness when irritation rises, choosing gentleness when tension builds, and choosing forgiveness when hurtful words slip out.

Paul reminds us that love has the power to hold relationships together. It strengthens unity when life grows complicated. It softens conflict before it grows. It helps couples stay patient and tenderhearted as they navigate the many seasons of marriage. When spouses choose love daily, they create a home where God's peace can flourish.

***

Choosing love daily is one of the most important habits in marriage. It sounds simple, but in real life this choice shapes how couples grow, how they heal, and how they hold on to one another through changing seasons. Love is not always the first emotion we feel in a busy household or a demanding workweek. Yet it can become the steady rhythm of a marriage when it is practiced intentionally.

Love grows when couples decide to act with patience in moments when impatience would be easier. It strengthens when husbands and wives offer encouraging words instead of criticism. It deepens when they slow down long enough to truly see each other's needs and respond with care. What makes love powerful is not only how it begins but how it continues, choice after choice, in both small and significant ways.

Some days choosing love means offering a gentle word after a stressful day. Other days it might mean apologizing first or giving your spouse the benefit of the doubt when emotions run high. On more difficult days it may involve forgiving a hurt or showing tenderness when your own heart feels tired. These acts may seem small, but they weave a marriage together with strength and stability.

We live in a culture that often celebrates emotion but neglects commitment. Scripture calls us to something deeper. Love in marriage is an ongoing decision that reflects God's steadfast love toward us. He loves us faithfully even when we struggle, and He invites us to love each other with that same steady heart.

Choosing love daily builds a marriage that feels safe. It nurtures trust because each spouse knows the other is willing to show up, even when life feels complicated. It allows both partners to relax into the relationship instead of bracing for disappointment. Over time, this consistent love creates an atmosphere where joy grows naturally.

Love also gives couples strength during seasons of hardship. When finances become strained, when illness enters the home, or when unexpected stress weighs heavily, daily love becomes a stabilizing force. It reminds each person that they are not alone. This steady commitment creates the kind of marriage where both spouses can rest knowing they are held, valued, and pursued with intention.

Marriage flourishes when choosing love becomes a daily practice rather than an occasional sentiment. God knows that love grows through action, which is why He calls us to put it on like clothing. When couples choose love with purpose, they cultivate a home that reflects His heart. They become a living testimony of His compassion and grace.

FROM HIS PERSPECTIVE

When I think about choosing love daily, I notice how often I rely on my feelings to decide how I respond. If I am tired, I withdraw. If I am stressed, I get impatient. These patterns show up before I even realize it. But when I pause and invite God into those moments, I feel my heart begin to shift. Love becomes less about emotion and more about intention.

There are days when choosing love means slowing down to listen even when my mind feels full. Other days it means giving Emeline a gentle response when my mood wants to go the other direction. I am learning that real love grows strongest when I choose it deliberately. And every time I make that choice, our marriage feels steadier, our home feels calmer, and I feel more connected to the man God is shaping me to be.

FROM HER PERSPECTIVE

This passage reminds me how easily small frustrations can build up in my heart. A long week, a messy house, or a stressful conversation can leave me feeling tense without even knowing why. When I do not choose love intentionally, those feelings can spill into my tone or my reactions. Yet when I pause and turn to the Lord, I remember the kind of wife I want to be.

Choosing love daily helps me slow down and respond with a softer spirit. It helps me see Emmett through eyes of tenderness rather than frustration. It reminds me that every day is a chance to create warmth in our home. When I choose love in small ways, I notice how quickly peace returns. I feel closer to my husband, more aligned with God, and more connected to the purpose He has for our marriage.

PRAYER

Lord, teach us to choose love in every season. Help us respond with patience, kindness, and gentleness even when life feels overwhelming. Fill our home with Your peace and guide our hearts to reflect Your love through our words and actions. Draw us closer to You and closer to each other each day. Amen.

CONVERSATION PROMPTS

1. When during the day do you feel most loved by me, and what specific actions or words make you feel supported and valued? How can we both be more intentional this week about choosing love even in moments when we feel tired, distracted, or overwhelmed?

2. What situations or emotions make it harder for you to respond with love, and how can I gently support you when those moments arise? How can we work together to create habits, rhythms, and conversations that help us choose love daily with greater consistency and joy?

CONNECTION PRACTICES

Choose one small way to show intentional love today through a kind word, a gentle gesture, or a helpful action. Later, sit together for five quiet minutes, holding hands and breathing slowly as you ask God to help you choose love throughout the week. Let the silence bring calm, closeness, and renewed intention as you enter the days ahead with tenderness and unity.

3. Grace for Imperfect People

"And be ye kind one to another, tenderhearted, forgiving one another, even as God for Christ's sake hath forgiven you."
Ephesians 4:32

A few years ago our close family friend Marissa shared a moment in her marriage that stayed with us. She and her husband, Chris, had been juggling two jobs, school schedules, and the usual busyness that comes with raising children. One evening, after an especially long day, Chris forgot to pick up their daughter from choir practice. Marissa had just settled into preparing dinner when the call came from the school office. She rushed out the door frustrated and embarrassed, feeling the weight of the day press a little harder.

When she arrived home, Chris immediately knew he had let her down. He tried to explain the mix up, but Marissa was too tired to hear it. She walked into the kitchen and saw the meal still sitting unfinished. In that quiet moment, she felt her shoulders drop. She realized how easily stress was steering her heart.

Instead of staying angry, she took a deep breath and whispered a short prayer. Chris followed her into the kitchen, ready for an argument, but she simply said, "It has been a hard day for both of us." His eyes filled with relief. That night they laughed, cooked together, and talked through the misunderstanding. Grace opened a door that frustration had nearly closed.

***

Ephesians 4:32 invites believers to be kind, tenderhearted, and forgiving toward one another, just as God has forgiven us through Christ. These words are simple, yet they speak directly into the daily rhythms of marriage. Paul is reminding the church that relationships flourish when hearts soften rather than harden. The call to kindness and tenderness is not a distant ideal. It is a daily practice.

In marriage, couples quickly learn that their imperfections will show up. There will be forgotten tasks, misunderstandings, emotional missteps, and moments of weakness. God knows this, which is why He anchors the command in His own forgiveness. We are asked to forgive because we have been forgiven. We are invited to be tenderhearted because God has shown tenderness toward us.

The verse describes a posture of the heart. Kindness slows our reactions. Tenderness listens before it assumes. Forgiveness clears the space where resentment tries to grow. Paul is teaching us that grace is not weakness. It is strength in its gentlest form. When spouses practice grace, they create a marriage environment where healing becomes possible and unity becomes stronger. Grace becomes the bridge that allows two imperfect people to walk toward one another again.

***

Grace in marriage is one of the most powerful gifts couples can give each other. It is not a dismissal of mistakes or a quiet endurance of unhealthy patterns. Instead, grace is a deliberate choice to respond with compassion when frustration tries to take over. It grows from an understanding that both spouses are learning, growing, and carrying burdens that are not always visible.

Every marriage encounters moments when grace becomes necessary. Sometimes it is needed after a careless word. Other times it is required after a forgotten responsibility or a difference in perspective. The truth is that marriage binds two imperfect people together, and imperfection requires gentleness. Without grace, small irritations can build into resentment. With grace, those same irritations become opportunities to strengthen trust and deepen love.

Grace allows room for missteps without letting them define the relationship. It gives the other person space to recover, rethink, and try again. When both spouses practice grace, the home becomes a safe place. Mistakes can be talked through instead of hidden. Weaknesses can be shared instead of masked. Growth happens naturally because the environment encourages honesty.

Grace also strengthens emotional intimacy. When a husband or wife responds with understanding rather than harshness, the other person feels valued. They feel safe enough to open up about fears, stresses, or concerns. This openness builds a deeper bond that cannot be manufactured through effort alone. Grace softens the heart and keeps communication gentle.

Yet grace does not mean avoiding boundaries or ignoring issues. True grace seeks healing. It allows couples to address problems with a calm, steady spirit instead of reacting in anger. Grace says, "We will work through this together," rather than, "You should have known better." It is the belief that the relationship is more important than the mistake.

Grace also reflects God's heart toward us. He does not give us what we deserve at our lowest moments. He meets us with mercy. In marriage, grace imitates this divine pattern. It turns conflict into conversation. It transforms tension into understanding. It reminds both spouses that love grows best in a climate of kindness.

When grace becomes part of daily life, marriage begins to feel lighter. Couples learn to extend patience even when emotions run high. They practice humility by admitting their own faults. They offer forgiveness not as a favor but as a gift that leads to peace. Over time, grace becomes woven into the foundation of the relationship, shaping it into something strong and beautiful.

Grace is not always easy, but it is always fruitful. It allows two imperfect people to build a marriage filled with compassion, healing, and lasting connection.

FROM HIS PERSPECTIVE

I have learned that my words carry more weight than I sometimes realize. When I am tired or distracted, I can speak too quickly or react without thinking. Later, I see the look in my wife's eyes and realize I missed a moment to be gentle. Grace helps me slow down. It reminds me that her heart matters more than my frustration. When she extends grace toward me, it softens me. It helps me listen better and respond with more tenderness. I am discovering that grace is not about ignoring mistakes. It is about choosing connection over pride. It is choosing to rebuild trust instead of pushing distance. Whenever I make that choice, our marriage feels warmer and safer. Grace helps me love her more like Christ loves me.

FROM HER PERSPECTIVE

There are moments when I feel overwhelmed and my reactions come out sharper than I intend. Later, I look back and wish I had paused. Grace gives me that pause. It helps me breathe before I speak and remember that my husband is trying too. When he offers me grace on difficult days, it feels like someone lifting a weight off my shoulders. It reminds me that we are on the same side. I am learning that giving grace is easier when I remember how deeply God has given grace to me. It helps me soften my heart instead of defending my pride. Each time I choose grace, I feel our marriage become more peaceful. It draws us closer and helps me love him with more patience and tenderness.

PRAYER

Lord, thank You for loving us with grace that never runs out. Help us reflect that same kindness toward each other. Teach us to slow our words, soften our reactions, and forgive quickly. Make our home a place where grace brings healing and draws our hearts closer together. Amen.

CONVERSATION PROMPTS

1. When do you feel most in need of grace from me, and what kinds of responses help your heart feel cared for rather than judged? How can we both create an atmosphere where grace is welcomed, practiced, and expected in the daily challenges we face as a couple?

2. What situations make it harder for you to offer grace, and how can we work together to slow down, communicate clearly, and support each other during those moments? How can we develop habits and rhythms that help grace become more natural in our marriage?

CONNECTION PRACTICES

When a minor frustration arises today, pause and respond with gentleness instead of irritation. Softening your tone brings unexpected peace. Later, each of you share one small area where you fell short this week. Offer a sincere apology and a sincere forgiveness without any explanations. Allow the moment to bring healing, understanding, and a quiet sense of closeness that strengthens the heart of your marriage.

4. Listening with the Heart

"Wherefore, my beloved brethren, let every man be swift to hear, slow to speak, slow to wrath."
James 1:19

A few months ago our longtime family friend Elijah shared something that humbled him. He and his wife, Naomi, had been married for more than twenty years. Their home was usually calm, but one evening Elijah came home distracted after a stressful day. Naomi began telling him about a difficult situation involving one of their children. She spoke with concern in her voice, hoping he would understand the weight of what she was feeling.

Elijah nodded while slipping off his shoes and checking a message on his phone. Naomi paused, waiting for him to look up. He did not. She finished her explanation quietly, feeling a little smaller than she had moments earlier. After a few minutes of silence she said softly, "I just needed you to hear me." That sentence stopped him.

He put down his phone, walked over to her, and asked her to tell the story again. This time he listened with his full attention. Naomi's shoulders relaxed as she talked. Later he told us, "I did not fix anything. All I did was listen, but it changed the whole evening."

It reminded us of something simple yet deeply important. Sometimes the greatest act of love is simply being fully present.

***

James 1:19 teaches believers to be quick to listen, slow to speak, and slow to anger. It is a verse most of us know, yet living it out takes intentional effort, especially in marriage. Listening comes first in the verse because it sets the tone for everything that follows. When we listen with care, we create space for understanding instead of misunderstanding. When we rush to speak, we often defend ourselves before hearing the heart of the person we love.

In marriage, listening with the heart means more than hearing words. It means paying attention to tone, emotion, and unspoken needs. It means showing interest even when we are tired and choosing presence even when we feel rushed. Listening tells your spouse, "You matter. Your feelings matter. Your thoughts matter."

James also connects listening to emotional restraint. When we slow our speech, emotions settle. Anger softens. Reactions become gentler. Listening becomes a way of loving with humility. God invites us to listen the way He listens to us, with patience and compassion.

Listening with the heart strengthens trust. It builds safety. It helps spouses connect deeply in ways that strengthen marriage through every season.

***

Listening is one of the most essential skills in marriage, yet it is also one of the easiest to overlook. Many couples talk often, but talking is not the same as listening. Listening means setting aside distractions, slowing down enough to understand, and giving your spouse the gift of your full attention. When we listen well, communication becomes clearer and the relationship becomes stronger.

Listening with the heart is more than a technique. It is an attitude of compassion. It recognizes that your spouse carries emotions, fears, memories, and pressures that may not be obvious at first glance. When a husband or wife feels truly heard, tension reduces and connection increases. They feel valued and understood, which creates a comfortable place for honesty.

Listening also helps prevent conflicts before they grow. Many disagreements happen not because of the issue itself but because one person felt unheard. When spouses listen before reacting, they avoid assumptions. They slow frustration before it rises. They understand the deeper meaning behind the words. This helps them respond in a way that builds the relationship rather than straining it.

Listening with the heart requires removing distractions. Phones, television, multitasking, and rushing through conversations can weaken connection. When couples choose to be fully present, even for a few minutes, conversations become richer. Little moments become opportunities for deep bonding.

Another part of listening is asking gentle questions. Instead of assuming intent, a simple question like "Can you help me understand what you are feeling?" can change the entire tone. It invites clarity rather than conflict. It shows humility. It communicates love.

Listening also means noticing the emotion behind the words. A spouse may say "I am fine" but their tone or silence may say something different. Listening with the heart pays attention to those deeper cues. It helps couples support each other with tenderness.

God listens to us with patience and compassion. He never rushes us or dismisses our thoughts. When we choose to listen like He does, we reflect His heart. Listening becomes an act of love, a spiritual practice, and a gift that transforms marriage.

Listening makes the home feel safe. It strengthens unity. It helps both people walk through life as a team instead of feeling alone. When couples practice listening with the heart, they create a marriage where understanding grows and connection becomes steady and strong.

FROM HIS PERSPECTIVE

Last week I came home tired from work. My mind was crowded with unfinished tasks and a hundred small worries. I walked into the living room and saw Emeline sitting on the couch, looking thoughtful. She said, "Can I talk to you about something that happened today?" I nodded, but I barely shifted my focus. I kept scrolling through an email, planning to listen and multitask.

She began sharing something that had upset her, and I murmured a few automatic responses. After a minute she stopped talking. I looked up and saw disappointment in her eyes. She said quietly, "I just wanted to feel like you were really here with me."

Her words stung because they were true. I set my phone down and said, "I am sorry. Please start again. I want to hear you." This time I leaned in, listened carefully, and asked questions. I could feel the difference in her posture. Her voice softened. Her shoulders relaxed.

When I listen well, our marriage feels warmer. When I listen poorly, distance grows quickly. I want her to know she has my full attention, not my divided focus. Listening is one of the clearest ways I can show love. It tells her she is valued, cherished, and never alone.

FROM HER PERSPECTIVE

Earlier this month I found myself overwhelmed after a long day. I sat at the kitchen table, sorting through bills while dinner simmered on the stove. When Emmett walked in, I said, "I think I am struggling more than I realized." He pulled out a chair and sat beside me. "Talk to me," he said.

I began explaining what had been weighing on me. Halfway through, my voice cracked. I expected him to reassure me quickly and move on, but instead he reached for my hand. "I am listening," he whispered. Something about the gentleness in his voice gave me permission to be honest. I told him how tired I felt, how stretched, and how worried I was about keeping up.

He nodded slowly, not interrupting. When he asked, "What do you need from me tonight?" I felt my eyes fill with tears. I said, "Just stay here with me for a minute." And he did.

That small conversation changed my whole evening. Listening is such a simple gift, but it fills the heart with comfort. It creates a safe place where I can be vulnerable without fear. I feel close to him in a way that strengthens our marriage more than anything else.

Listening is love in its quietest form, and it continues to draw us closer every day.

PRAYER

Lord, help us listen to each other with tender hearts. Teach us to slow our reactions, quiet our distractions, and give each other our full attention. Fill our home with understanding, compassion, and gentle communication. Guide our conversations so they bring unity and draw us closer to You and to one another. Amen.

CONVERSATION PROMPTS

1. When do you feel most listened to by me, and what makes those moments meaningful to your heart? How can we each create more space for focused attention, patient conversation, and deeper understanding throughout our week, especially when life feels busy or overwhelming?

2. What distractions or habits make it harder for us to listen well to each other, and how can we work together to remove or reduce those barriers? What simple changes could help us practice listening with the heart in a way that strengthens our unity and emotional closeness?

CONNECTION PRACTICES

Take ten minutes together with no screens or distractions. One spouse shares freely for five minutes while the other listens with full attention, then switch. Before bed, ask gently, "What is something on your mind today that you want me to understand" and listen without interruption. These simple moments of attentive presence create emotional safety and invite deeper connection.

5. Speaking Life over Each Other

"Death and life are in the power of the tongue:
and they that love it shall eat the fruit thereof."
Proverbs 18:21

Years ago, Christian author and pastor Gary Smalley shared a moment from his early marriage that transformed how he communicated with his wife, Norma. During a season when ministry responsibilities consumed him, he began noticing that Norma smiled less often. She went about her work faithfully, but something in her spirit seemed weighed down.

One evening he made an offhand remark about something she had forgotten to do. He did not mean it harshly, but he saw how her expression dimmed. She paused, folding a towel in her hands, and whispered, "Sometimes it feels like you only see what I get wrong."

He said her words pierced his heart. He had been unaware of how his tone was shaping the atmosphere of their home. That night he asked God to help him speak with tenderness and encouragement. Over the next weeks he began expressing gratitude, noticing the good, and offering life giving words.

He later wrote that those simple changes brought warmth back into their home in ways no grand gesture ever had. Words, he learned, were shaping their marriage far more than he realized.

***

Proverbs 18:21 teaches that life and death are in the power of the tongue. Words are never neutral. They can nourish or wither, strengthen or discourage, calm or aggravate. This wisdom speaks directly into marriage, where daily communication holds tremendous influence.

Our tone often carries more weight than the actual words spoken. A gentle comment can soothe a weary heart, while a careless remark can echo longer than intended. Scripture tells us that our speech reveals the posture of our heart. When we speak life, we align our communication with God's character. When we speak harshly, we risk planting seeds of insecurity or resentment.

Speaking life does not mean avoiding truth or discomfort. It means expressing what needs to be said with grace. It means noticing the good, affirming effort, and offering kindness even when emotions run high. Words that bring life strengthen unity, deepen trust, and nurture emotional closeness.

In marriage, God invites us to use words the way He uses them, bringing encouragement, healing, and hope.

***

Speaking life over each other is a practice that shapes the environment of the home every single day. Husbands and wives often underestimate how deeply their words affect the emotional climate around them. A sentence spoken with gentleness can be remembered for years, just as a careless phrase can leave a lingering ache.

Speaking life is a conscious choice. It means deciding to affirm rather than criticize. It means expressing gratitude for the things your spouse does that often go unnoticed. It means offering encouragement when your spouse feels insecure or weary. Over time, these habits fill the relationship with warmth and safety.

This practice also strengthens trust. When a spouse consistently hears words of appreciation and affirmation, they feel secure. They open up more freely. Vulnerability becomes easier because they know their heart will be handled gently. Even difficult conversations become more productive when the relationship is rooted in life giving communication.

Speaking life is a way of partnering with God. Jesus spoke words that restored, uplifted, and called out potential. He used speech to strengthen those He loved. When spouses follow His example, they cultivate peace in their marriage.

Life giving words also help couples navigate stress. When days become heavy, a sincere "I am proud of you," or "I appreciate you," can bring renewed strength. These simple phrases can reset the tone of an entire evening.

This does not mean ignoring problems. It means handling them with kindness, clarity, and respect. Speaking life builds a foundation where even conflict can lead to deeper unity.

A marriage shaped by encouraging words becomes a place where both spouses thrive. There is room for joy, healing, and emotional closeness. Speaking life turns ordinary conversations into opportunities for blessing, strengthening the bond day after day.

FROM HIS PERSPECTIVE

Earlier this week I walked through the door feeling drained. I dropped my bag, rubbed my forehead, and let out a long breath. Emeline looked up and simply said, "I am glad you are home. I missed you today."

Those words softened me instantly.

Later that night I found myself thinking about the way I speak to her. I realized how quickly I default to practical words about schedules or responsibilities and how easily I forget the words that bring life. When I told her, "I appreciate how much you carry for our family," something in her expression brightened. It reminded me that encouragement is not complicated. It is intentional.

My words create the atmosphere of our home. When I speak gently, our connection feels easier. When I speak encouragement, her heart opens. I am learning to use my voice as a way to love her, to support her, and to lift her spirit. Speaking life is one of the clearest ways I can honor her.

FROM HER PERSPECTIVE

I have become more aware of how my words shape the way Emmett feels when he walks through the door. Sometimes I speak quickly because I am tired, and I see how it affects him. Other times I slow down and choose gentler words, and the whole tone of our evening changes. It reminds me that life giving words are not dramatic speeches. They are quiet seeds planted throughout the day.

I want our home to feel like a place where he is safe and appreciated. When I tell him how much I respect the way he leads or how grateful I am for his efforts, I see peace settle on his face. Speaking life also softens my own heart. It reminds me to look for the good, to notice the effort, and to value the small things he does for our family.

I want my words to reflect God's heart toward him. I want to strengthen him, not wear him down. Speaking life is a practice I am learning day by day, and I can already see how it draws us closer.

PRAYER

Lord, help us use our words with tenderness and wisdom. Teach us to speak encouragement, gratitude, and truth that brings life into our home. Guard our hearts from harshness and fill our mouths with kindness. Make our marriage a place where Your love is heard through the way we speak. Amen.

CONVERSATION PROMPTS

1. What kinds of words help you feel supported, valued, and understood, and how can I practice using them more intentionally? How do life giving words influence the closeness and peace you feel in our marriage?

2. What comments or tones feel discouraging to you, even if unintentional, and how can we gently help each other replace those patterns with words that bring comfort, clarity, and unity? How can we remind each other lovingly when we slip?

CONNECTION PRACTICES

Each spouse shares three sincere, specific statements of appreciation or encouragement. Speak slowly, making each sentence meaningful. Then pray aloud for one another, asking God to strengthen, guide, and encourage your spouse with His love. Let the prayer be simple and heartfelt. These practices nurture gratitude and spiritual closeness, lifting the atmosphere of your marriage.

6. Forgiveness and Reconciliation

“For if ye forgive men their trespasses,
your heavenly Father will also forgive you.”
Matthew 6:14

One Saturday morning, our daughter Paldy came into the kitchen looking frustrated. She had been working on a school project late the night before, and in her tiredness she had borrowed her mom’s tablet without asking. In the rush of getting ready for bed, she left it on the couch. Paldy accidentally knocked it over, cracking the corner of the screen.

When Emeline saw the damage the next morning, she let out a sigh. Paldy, froze, guilt written all over her face. She whispered, “I am really sorry. I should have asked.” Her mom paused, took a breath, and nodded slowly. For a moment it looked like the day would begin with tension.

But then I stepped in gently. I said, “Accidents can be fixed. What matters most is honesty and how we move forward.” Emeline’s eyes softened. She leaned into her mom and repeated her apology, this time with relief in her voice. Her mom wrapped her in a hug and said, “I forgive you. Thank you for telling the truth.”

The tone of the whole day changed. The forgiveness offered in that small moment lifted the weight off everyone’s hearts and brought peace back into their home.

***

When we forgive others, God forgives us. Jesus speaks these words in the context of prayer, reminding us that forgiveness is not separate from our relationship with Him. It is part of our spiritual posture. He invites us to extend the same grace we have received.

In marriage, forgiveness becomes essential because two people, no matter how deeply they love each other, will eventually hurt one another. Misunderstandings, harsh tones, forgotten responsibilities, and emotional missteps are part of life together. Forgiveness does not ignore the hurt, but it releases the grip of resentment.

Reconciliation goes beyond forgiveness. It restores closeness. It turns toward the other person instead of pulling away. It builds a path back to unity where division tried to grow.

Jesus teaches that forgiveness flows from a heart shaped by God’s mercy. When we remember how greatly God has forgiven us, it becomes easier to soften our reactions and extend grace to our spouse. In marriage, forgiveness is not an occasional event but an ongoing practice that protects connection and nurtures peace.

***

Forgiveness and reconciliation form the backbone of a strong marriage. Couples who learn to practice forgiveness consistently create an environment where love can flourish despite human weakness. Forgiveness does not excuse wrong behavior, nor does it erase the impact of hurtful words or actions. Instead, it opens a door for healing and allows both spouses to begin again with a renewed heart.

Forgiveness requires humility. It requires recognizing that neither spouse is perfect and that grace must flow in both directions. It also requires patience, because sometimes emotions need time to settle before forgiveness can be offered wholeheartedly. Yet forgiveness remains essential because without it, pain accumulates silently and distance grows in small, unnoticed increments.

Reconciliation completes the process. It brings hearts back together by repairing what was strained. This step includes honest conversation, gentle explanation of the hurt, and a willingness to rebuild trust. When reconciliation follows forgiveness, intimacy returns. The relationship becomes stronger than before because the couple has weathered a storm together with grace.

Forgiveness also protects the home from becoming a place of silent resentment. Couples who forgive quickly find it easier to laugh together, to communicate openly, and to enjoy the ordinary rhythms of life without tension clouding the atmosphere.

God models forgiveness for us. He offers mercy freely, repeatedly, and fully. When couples mirror His heart, they turn their marriage into a living picture of His kindness. Forgiveness becomes part of the daily rhythm, not something saved for dramatic conflicts. Even small irritations can be softened by quick, sincere apologies and gentle releases of frustration.

A forgiving marriage is a joyful marriage. It allows both people to relax into love without fear of lingering condemnation. It nurtures emotional safety and creates a home where reconciliation feels natural and welcome. Through forgiveness, couples discover the steady peace God desires for their relationship.

FROM HIS PERSPECTIVE

A few nights ago, Emeline and I found ourselves in one of those small misunderstandings that grow bigger than intended. I made a comment that came out sharper than I meant, and I saw her expression drop immediately. I said, "I did not mean it like that." She responded calmly, "I know, but it still stung."

Later that evening, after the kids were in bed, I sat next to her on the couch and said quietly, "I am sorry for how I spoke earlier." She looked at me for a moment, then nodded and said, "Thank you. I forgive you."

That simple exchange brought relief. I could feel something settle inside me. Forgiveness is powerful because it clears the space between us. I would rather apologize a hundred times than let hurt grow in silence.

I am learning that forgiveness is not about proving I am right. It is about protecting the closeness we share. When I humble myself and ask for forgiveness, I feel more connected to her. And when she forgives me, I am reminded of the grace God has given both of us.

Forgiveness makes marriage lighter. It keeps love clear and strong. It opens the way for peace to return quickly.

FROM HER PERSPECTIVE

Forgiveness is something I am learning to practice with both honesty and softness. When Emmett hurts my feelings, even unintentionally, I can feel my heart tighten. My instinct is to retreat for a moment, to protect myself. But when I pause and bring it to the Lord, I hear a gentle reminder that grace heals more than withdrawal ever could.

Forgiving him helps me stay connected rather than guarded. It allows me to see his heart instead of focusing on the momentary hurt. When he apologizes sincerely, I feel invited back into closeness. And when I choose forgiveness even before he fully understands how I felt, I notice my own heart becoming more tender and more aligned with God's love.

Reconciliation means turning toward Emmett, not away. It means allowing peace to settle where tension was trying to take hold. I am grateful for a marriage where we can apologize, forgive, and begin again as many times as needed. That rhythm keeps our hearts soft and our home peaceful.

PRAYER

Lord, teach us to forgive quickly and wholeheartedly. Help us release hurt with grace and choose reconciliation over distance. Fill our home with peace as we reflect Your mercy toward each other. Restore unity whenever tension arises and guide our hearts with compassion. Amen.

CONVERSATION PROMPTS

1. What kinds of situations make you feel most hurt or misunderstood, and how can I be more attentive to those tender places in your heart? How can we approach moments of offense in ways that protect connection and lead us toward reconciliation instead of distance?

2. What helps you forgive more easily, and what makes forgiveness harder for you? How can we create habits that make forgiveness a natural rhythm in our marriage, including gentle communication, timely apologies, and shared prayer?

CONNECTION PRACTICES

Hold hands and speak one sentence of prayer for each other, asking God to meet the quiet needs of your spouse's heart. Later, write a brief prayer note and place it somewhere your spouse will find it. It can be on a pillow, in a coat pocket, or beside a morning cup. These small spiritual gestures create warmth, reassurance, and a sense of being lovingly seen.

7. Praying for Each Other

"And this I pray, that your love may abound
yet more and more in knowledge and in all judgment."
Philippians 1:9

One of the most remarkable stories from George Müller's journals is the way he prayed for five specific friends to come to Christ. He prayed for them daily, never skipping a morning, never discouraged by silence. Within a few months the first became a believer. Five years later, the second surrendered to Christ. Six more years passed before the third followed.

The final two took much longer. One trusted Christ shortly before Müller died. The last came to faith a few years after Müller's passing. Sixty years of prayer, steady and unwavering, finally brought all five to salvation.

Müller always said prayer was not persuading God but partnering with Him. He believed prayer was part of love. Prayer kept his heart soft, his faith steady, and his compassion alive, even when nothing visible happened.

His story reminds us that praying for the people we love will always matter. God hears every whisper and stores every petition in His faithfulness.

***

EXPLANATION OF THE PASSAGE

Philippians 1:9 shows Paul praying intentionally for the spiritual growth of believers he loved. He prayed that their love would grow in knowledge and discernment, knowing that spiritual maturity flows from a heart shaped by God.

Paul prayed because he knew human strength is not enough. Prayer brings God's wisdom to tired minds, God's comfort to discouraged hearts, and God's clarity to confused seasons. In marriage, prayer becomes a steady anchor. It softens words, slows anger, nurtures patience, and restores tenderness.

When spouses pray for each other, they invite the Holy Spirit to work in places where their own efforts fall short. They cultivate humility by admitting their dependence on God. And they express love in one of the most powerful ways Scripture teaches: lifting each other before the Father.

***

Praying for each other strengthens marriage in ways nothing else can. Prayer protects the heart from bitterness, fear, and isolation. It brings God's peace into the home and helps spouses stand together rather than drift apart.

Scripture repeatedly reinforces why prayer is essential for relationships. James 5:16 teaches that the prayers of the righteous are "powerful and effective." When a husband or wife prays for their spouse, they are calling on God's strength, not their own. They are inviting divine wisdom into daily life.

Prayer also softens the heart. Ezekiel 36:26 says God can remove a heart of stone and give a heart of flesh. Many marital tensions arise from hardened emotions, but prayer opens the door for God to soften attitudes, shift perspectives, and bring new tenderness.

Prayer helps spouses carry each other's burdens. Galatians 6:2 tells us to "bear one another's burdens," and lifting those burdens before God is one of the most loving ways to do this. When one spouse feels overwhelmed, the other can partner with God to bring support, peace, and renewed strength.

Prayer builds unity. Matthew 18:19 shows the power of two people agreeing together before God. When a couple prays for the same things, they align their hearts in purpose. Even if they feel disconnected, prayer gradually draws them closer. It is difficult to stay resentful toward someone you are actively praying for.

Prayer also brings clarity. Proverbs 3:5 to 6 teaches that God directs the paths of those who trust Him. When spouses pray for one another, they invite God to guide decisions, soften words, and shape their responses.

Prayer guards marriage. Philippians 4:6 to 7 promises that God's peace will guard our hearts when we bring everything to Him. Marriage needs guarding. Stress, misunderstandings, and unspoken worries can build walls very quickly. But prayer opens a gate for peace to enter and stay.

Above all, prayer reminds couples that God is part of their story. He sees their efforts, hears their cries, and responds with grace. A praying marriage becomes a steady marriage, held together not only by love but by the presence of God Himself.

FROM HIS PERSPECTIVE

A few nights ago I sat on the edge of the bed, listening to my wife breathe slowly after a long day. I whispered a simple prayer, "Lord, give her rest and peace tonight." It was short, but something peaceful filled me the moment I prayed it.

The next morning I told her, "I prayed for you last night." She smiled in that quiet way she does when something touches her deeply. It reminded me again how prayer strengthens more than the moment. It strengthens the bond between us.

Praying for her changes my attitude. I notice her needs more. I become slower to frustration and quicker to compassion. When I lift her before God, I feel humility rising and pride fading. Prayer helps me love her the way Scripture calls me to love, from a place of patience and spiritual strength.

FROM HER PERSPECTIVE

Last week I was carrying worries I had not talked about yet. I felt stretched thin, and my thoughts were scattered. Emmett walked into the kitchen and said quietly, "I prayed for you on my way home."

Those words made my whole body relax. I said, "Thank you. I needed that more than I even knew."

That moment reminded me how powerful it is to be prayed for, not just loved but lifted to God. When he prays for me, I feel seen, supported, and deeply valued. Prayer connects us in a way that conversation alone cannot. It makes the day feel lighter and the burden feel shared.

Knowing he prays for me gives me a kind of peace that settles slowly and stays.

PRAYER

Lord, teach us to lift each other before You with sincerity and compassion. Help our prayers become a source of strength, peace, and unity in our home. Shape our hearts through prayer and draw us closer to Your presence and to each other. Amen.

CONVERSATION PROMPTS

1. What is one area of your life where you feel most in need of prayer right now, and how can I bring that request before God with patience, care, and consistency this week? How does it help your heart when you know your spouse is praying for you?

2. What types of prayers strengthen you the most, and how can we build a gentle rhythm of praying for each other that fits naturally into our week? How can prayer help us stay spiritually connected through seasons of stress, joy, change, or challenge?

CONNECTION PRACTICES

Hold hands and pause together, each speaking one simple sentence of prayer for the other's heart and needs. Keep it gentle and sincere. Later in the day, write a short prayer note and place it somewhere your spouse will find it, allowing the words to quietly encourage them. These small acts of shared prayer create warmth, deepen spiritual closeness, and remind both of you that God is present in your everyday moments together.

8. Strengthening Emotional Intimacy

"Rejoice with them that do rejoice,
and weep with them that weep."
Romans 12:15

One night after youth group, Paldy came home quieter than usual. She walked into the living room, tucked her knees under her, and leaned against the corner of the couch. Her mom joined her and simply asked, "Hard night?" Paldy nodded, tears welling. Someone had made a comment that stung deeply, and she had held it in until she walked through the front door.

Her mom wrapped an arm around her, and a few moments later her dad came in, took one look at them, and sat on her other side. He did not ask for details. He did not try to cheer her up quickly. He just rested a hand on her back and said, "We are with you."

The tension in her face softened almost immediately.

Later that evening her parents said to one another, "She opened her heart because she felt safe." That simple moment reminded them that emotional intimacy is made in those quiet, gentle places where hearts feel understood.

***

Romans 12:15 invites us to "weep with those who weep and rejoice with those who rejoice." Emotional intimacy grows when couples do exactly that. It becomes strong not because two people never struggle, but because they enter each other's feelings with compassion.

The heart does not open quickly to a spouse who rushes or corrects too fast. Proverbs 20:5 reminds us that a person's heart is like deep waters, and drawing those waters out requires insight, patience, and gentleness. Emotional intimacy grows when we honor those deep waters rather than force them.

Galatians 6:2 teaches us to "carry each other's burdens," and emotional closeness becomes possible when burdens are shared instead of hidden. Empathy makes space for slow explanations, fragile feelings, and honest conversations. It communicates, "Your heart matters to me. I want to understand, even when the feelings are messy or quiet."

Scripture draws a picture of emotional intimacy as the steady practice of entering one another's joys and sorrows with kindness. This is how hearts knit together in lasting ways.

***

Emotional intimacy is the quiet strength of a marriage. It is what helps two people feel connected even in seasons when life is busy or demanding. The Bible speaks often about compassion, gentleness, and patience, all of which are the soil where emotional intimacy grows. Colossians 3:12 calls believers to clothe themselves with these very qualities. When a husband and wife practice them intentionally, their home becomes a place where vulnerability feels safe.

Emotional intimacy requires listening without rushing. It requires seeing your spouse's tone or expression as an invitation to lean closer, not step away. Little questions like "Tell me more," or "What are you feeling right now?" open doors that otherwise remain shut. Trust deepens each time one spouse shows interest in the inner world of the other.

It also grows through shared burdens. When one spouse feels overwhelmed or discouraged, emotional intimacy says, "I will carry this moment with you." This echoes the teaching in Galatians 6:2, not mechanically but naturally, because closeness thrives where burdens are lifted together.

There is also joy in emotional intimacy. When a spouse celebrates even small victories, the other joins in wholeheartedly. This reflects the first half of Romans 12:15, the call to rejoice with those who rejoice. Marriage becomes richer when both the heavy and the light moments are shared.

Emotional intimacy is spiritual as well as emotional. It reflects the way God draws near to His people with tenderness. As couples practice empathy, compassion, and understanding, they reflect His heart inside their home. Their marriage becomes a safe refuge where love deepens through authenticity and gentle presence.

FROM HIS PERSPECTIVE (WITH SHORT STORY)

Last week, as we sat on the sofa after the kids had gone upstairs, I noticed my wife staring at her hands. I asked softly, "What is going on in your heart?" She hesitated, then said, "I feel stretched thin, and I do not even know why."

Instead of offering a plan to fix it, I moved closer and said, "Let me sit with you in it." That was all it took. She leaned her head on my shoulder and let out a long breath.

I am realizing emotional intimacy grows when I do less speaking and more listening. When I make room for her feelings, however tangled or quiet they are, she opens up. What she needs most on those evenings is not a solution, but safety. And safety comes from presence, gentleness, and patience.

When she allows me to see her heart, I consider it a deep honor. Emotional closeness makes our marriage feel steady and warm. It helps me love her the way God calls me to love, not just in action but in tenderness.

FROM HER PERSPECTIVE

Emotional intimacy grows when I let myself be honest with my husband instead of trying to appear strong all the time. Some evenings I feel overwhelmed for reasons I cannot explain, and when I finally say, "I am not okay tonight," something inside me softens. His reaction makes all the difference. When he looks at me with understanding instead of impatience, I feel safe enough to keep talking.

I am learning that emotional closeness requires courage. It means sharing the deeper layers of my heart. It means saying the truth even when I feel vulnerable. Each time he listens with gentleness, my trust deepens. Emotional intimacy becomes a place where I can rest, breathe, and feel supported.

I want us to keep creating those quiet, honest moments. They strengthen our marriage more than anything else. They remind me that we are not just living life side by side, but heart to heart.

PRAYER

Lord, teach us to enter each other's feelings with compassion and patience. Help us listen with tenderness, understand without rushing, and create an environment where both of our hearts feel safe. Draw us closer in emotional intimacy as we follow Your way of gentleness. Amen.

CONVERSATION PROMPTS

1. When do you find it hardest to share your deeper feelings with me, and what would make it easier for you to open up in those moments? How can I respond in a way that helps you feel truly safe, valued, and understood instead of rushed or dismissed?

2. Can you remember a specific time when you felt deeply understood by me, even more than you expected? What did I do or say in that moment that helped you feel seen, and how can we intentionally create more moments like that in our everyday life together?

CONNECTION PRACTICES

Share one emotion you each felt today and briefly explain what led to it. Do not offer advice or solutions, only presence and understanding. After sharing, spend five minutes giving comfort through gentle touch, a soft tone, or warm words without trying to fix anything. Let the moment be simple and calm. Allow this quiet exchange to ease tension, deepen empathy, and draw your hearts closer in a way that feels warm and safe.

9. Strengthening Physical Intimacy

"Let the husband render unto the wife due benevolence: and likewise also the wife unto the husband."
1 Corinthians 7:3

In their early years of marriage, before Emeline and her brother were born, evenings looked very different. The couple remembers one night after a long, tiring week. He felt ready for closeness, longing for that physical connection that reminded him they were more than teammates. She, however, felt emotionally drained, carrying a week's worth of worries in her shoulders.

As they climbed into bed, he reached for her hand and tried to move closer. She paused and said quietly, "I love you, but my heart feels tired tonight. I want to be close, but I feel overwhelmed."

In the past, that kind of moment might have turned into hurt feelings or unspoken tension. That night, he took a different path. He gently squeezed her hand and said, "Then let me just hold you. No expectations. I just want you to rest."

She exhaled, almost in relief, and leaned into him. They lay there in the quiet, talking softly for a while. The pressure she had felt around intimacy began to fade, replaced by safety and tenderness.

Later they realized something important. Physical intimacy flourishes when it grows out of emotional security, kindness, and patient love.

***

In 1 Corinthians 7:3, Paul urges husbands and wives to care for one another in their physical relationship with mutual concern, not selfish demand. This passage reminds us that intimacy is not about taking, but about giving and serving each other in love.

God's original design in Genesis 2:24 describes marriage as two becoming "one flesh." This union is not only physical. It expresses trust, vulnerability, and covenant commitment. Physical intimacy is a powerful way that unity is expressed and renewed within marriage.

The beauty of this design is portrayed poetically in the Song of Solomon, where affection, desire, and tenderness are celebrated within the safety of covenant love. There, intimacy is woven together with respect, delight, and mutual pursuit.

Together, these passages show that physical intimacy is sacred and relational. It is meant to be a place of comfort, joy, and unity, shaped by love and gentle care.

***

Strengthening physical intimacy begins with honoring God's design and honoring each other. When a husband and wife approach intimacy with mutual respect and kindness, they mirror the heart behind 1 Corinthians 7:3. Closeness becomes something shared, not demanded. It becomes a gift that both can enjoy, not a duty weighed down with pressure.

Unity in Genesis 2:24 is more than a moment. It is a picture of ongoing oneness, expressed emotionally, spiritually, and physically. Physical intimacy becomes richer when those other areas are nurtured. A listening ear, a gentle word, or a simple act of service earlier in the day often makes closeness at night feel more natural and desired.

The tender imagery of Song of Solomon hints that intimacy grows where there is delight, affirmation, and patience. It does not rush. It invites. It cherishes. It speaks kindly. In marriage today, that means slowing down enough to understand each other's needs and fears, talking openly about what helps each person feel safe, and honoring each other's boundaries.

Some couples carry past wounds, insecurities, or fears into the marriage bed. God sees those places and cares about them. He does not shame weakness. Instead, He invites healing over time through prayer, patient conversation, and sometimes wise counsel. As trust grows, intimacy can become a place of healing rather than anxiety.

Physical intimacy is a gift, not a test. When husbands and wives pursue it with humility and gentleness, they reflect the love of Christ in a very personal way. Closeness becomes something that restores, reassures, and renews their covenant.

***

FROM HIS PERSPECTIVE

When I look at the men around me, I notice a common theme. Many of them deeply desire physical closeness in their marriage, but do not always know how to talk about it. Behind the jokes or casual comments, there is often a quiet ache for connection, not just physically, but emotionally as well.

Some men feel guilty for wanting intimacy but are unsure how to express it without sounding demanding. Others feel discouraged when they sense distance, but they keep it inside rather than risk rejection. Underneath all of that, I think many of us simply want to feel wanted, not just needed.

I am learning that if we, as men, want intimacy to grow, we must help create an atmosphere where our wives feel safe and cherished. When we practice patience, when we listen to their hearts, when we show affection without always expecting it to lead further, we build trust. And in that trust, physical closeness often becomes easier, more joyful, and more deeply satisfying for both of us.

FROM HER PERSPECTIVE

For a long time, intimacy felt complicated for me. There were confusing experiences in my childhood that left me feeling unsafe in my own skin. Even though nothing in our marriage was threatening, those old memories lingered like shadows I could not name. I loved my husband, but there were seasons when physical closeness stirred fear instead of comfort.

I remember quietly asking God, "Why does something meant to be beautiful feel so heavy for me?" Slowly, He began to untangle the knots in my heart. He used His Word, gentle friends, and the steady kindness of my husband to remind me that intimacy in marriage is meant to be safe, tender, and honoring.

My husband's patience became a huge part of that healing. When he told me, "We will move at the pace that feels safe for you," something inside me relaxed. I did not feel pressured. I felt valued. Over time, with many conversations and many prayers,

God softened those fearful places.

I would not say every struggle vanished in a moment, but I can say that today intimacy feels far more like a gift and far less like a battle. God has been kind to show me that He can redeem even the tender, vulnerable parts of my story.

PRAYER

Lord, thank You for designing intimacy as a gift within marriage. Help us to approach each other with gentleness, patience, and honor. Heal any hidden wounds or fears that make closeness difficult. Teach us to love each other well, so that our physical intimacy reflects Your tenderness and faithfulness. Amen.

CONVERSATION PROMPTS

1. What helps you feel most safe and comfortable when it comes to physical closeness, and what makes it more difficult for you? How can I better support you, emotionally and practically, so that intimacy feels like a place of peace and not pressure in our marriage?

2. Are there parts of your past, your body image, or your emotional world that affect how you experience intimacy today, even if you have never fully explained them? How can we gently talk about those things together, inviting God into the conversation and responding to each other with compassion and patience?

CONNECTION PRACTICES

Set aside ten quiet minutes to simply be close with no expectations attached. Hold hands, sit together, or cuddle in a way that feels safe and comforting. Afterward, each of you share one thing you appreciate about the other's approach to intimacy and offer one reassurance such as, "You are safe with me," or "Your comfort matters to me." Let these moments create warmth, safety, and a deeper sense of trust between you.

10. Navigating Conflict with Wisdom

"Wherefore, my beloved brethren, let every man be swift to hear, slow to speak, slow to wrath,"
James 1:19

One of the most famous true stories about reveals how he handled conflict with remarkable humility. During the Civil War, a Union officer made a harsh and inaccurate remark about President Abraham Lincoln's leadership. The comment spread quickly, and several men urged Lincoln to remove the officer for disrespect.

Instead of reacting with anger or authority, Lincoln quietly asked to meet with the officer privately.

When the man entered his office, he braced himself for harsh consequences. Instead, Lincoln shook his hand and said, "I have heard what was said. I believe you spoke from frustration, not from your true judgment. Tell me what weighs on your mind."

The officer stood stunned. He had expected rebuke. Instead, he was invited into conversation. As he explained the discouragement pressing on him, Lincoln listened with calm patience. The officer later wrote that Lincoln's gentleness "disarmed" him and filled him with loyalty.

Lincoln's ability to stay calm, listen deeply, and respond with wisdom turned a potential rupture into reconciliation.

That moment teaches us something deeply relevant to marriage. Conflict becomes transformative when humility takes the lead.

***

James 1:19 urges believers to be "quick to listen, slow to speak, and slow to become angry." This is not only good advice; it is spiritual wisdom. Conflict handled with this posture becomes a doorway to understanding rather than division.

Proverbs 15:1 adds that "a gentle answer turns away wrath," reflecting the very approach Lincoln used and the approach that softens tense moments in a marriage. When gentleness enters a heated conversation, anger loses its grip and clarity begins to rise.

Romans 12:18 offers another guiding truth: "If it is possible, as far as it depends on you, live at peace with everyone." Peace is not always immediate, but Scripture calls us to pursue it intentionally, especially with the person closest to us.

Together, these verses shape a way of navigating conflict that honors God and protects the unity of the home.

***

Every married couple faces conflict. What makes a marriage strong is not the absence of disagreement but the presence of wisdom and humility within it. James 1:19 gives us a roadmap—listen first, speak second, and let anger settle rather than surge. When spouses practice this, they give each other space to express emotion safely.

Proverbs 15:1 reminds us how powerful tone can be. A harsh word can escalate a minor issue into a relational wound, but a gentle response can soften even difficult conversations. Gentleness does not avoid truth; it delivers truth in a way the heart can receive.

Romans 12:18 encourages believers to pursue peace in every relationship, and marriage is at the very center of that calling. Pursuing peace does not mean avoiding issues. It means talking through them with humility, patience, and a willingness to understand.

Healthy conflict includes:

- Asking questions instead of making assumptions
- Listening without planning your rebuttal
- Naming emotions instead of attacking character
- Seeking understanding before demanding agreement
- Taking breaks when emotions become overwhelming
- Returning with a calmer spirit and a willingness to reconcile

Conflict becomes destructive when spouses fight to win. It becomes redemptive when they seek to understand. When couples follow biblical wisdom—quick to listen, slow to speak, and slow to anger—they create an environment where conflict becomes a catalyst for growth rather than division.

FROM HIS PERSPECTIVE

I have noticed something among men I know, and honestly in myself too. Many of us struggle with conflict not because we want to fight, but because we do not always know how to express our emotions calmly. When we feel disrespected or misunderstood, our instinct is often to defend, shut down, or get louder. It takes real strength to slow down instead.

Men around me often admit they wish they could handle conflict with more patience. They want to understand their wives better. They want to respond with calm rather than frustration. But old habits rise quickly.

I am learning that humility is not weakness. It is wisdom. When I pause before reacting, when I listen without interrupting, when I choose gentleness over defensiveness, our marriage becomes more peaceful. Conflict becomes a place of closeness rather than distance.

And I see the same change in other men who choose humility. When husbands lead with calm steadiness, the entire tone of the home shifts. That is the kind of man I want to be.

FROM HER PERSPECTIVE

Growing up, conflict felt unsafe for me. There were raised voices, slammed doors, and long silences that lasted days. As a child I often felt responsible for soothing tension I could not possibly fix. Those experiences shaped how I reacted to conflict later in life. Even as an adult, raised tones could make my heart race.

In marriage, this became a real struggle. When my husband and I disagreed, I sometimes panicked inside. Not because he was harsh, but because old memories whispered lies. I would withdraw, or cry unexpectedly, or shut down completely.

I remember praying, "Lord, please teach me a new way." Slowly, He did. God used His Word to steady me and my husband's calm presence to retrain my heart. When my husband said, "We are on the same team," something inside me softened each time. His patience helped me unlearn fear.

Today conflict still feels tender, but it no longer feels frightening. God has been healing the childhood places where fear lived. Our marriage has become the safe place where I am learning that disagreement does not end love, and tension does not equal danger. It is a slow transformation, but it is real.

PRAYER

Lord, teach us to approach conflict with humility, gentleness, and wisdom. Make us slow to anger, quick to listen, and patient in speech. Heal any wounds that make conflict frightening or overwhelming. Guide us toward peace, unity, and grace in every hard moment. Amen.

CONVERSATION PROMPTS

1. When conflict arises, what helps you feel safe, calm, and heard? What actions or tones from me make resolution easier, and what makes it harder? How can we create a shared approach to conflict that protects connection even in heated moments?

2. Are there moments from your past, your personality, or your stress patterns that influence how you react during conflict? How can we support each other with compassion in those vulnerable areas and work together toward emotional steadiness?

CONNECTION PRACTICES

If emotions rise too quickly, either of you may ask for a five minute pause. Step away, breathe, and pray separately, then return with calmer spirits and a willingness to listen. Once this week, if tension starts to build, pause together and say, "We are on the same team." Let those words reset the moment, helping you approach the issue with unity instead of opposition, strengthening connection and emotional steadiness.

11. Building Trust through Consistency

"Most men will proclaim every one his
own goodness: but a faithful man who can find?"
Proverbs 20:6

Ethan and Lily had been married for twelve years when they hit a season that quietly tested their trust. It began with small things. Ethan promised he would be home early but got caught up at work and forgot to text. Lily said she would handle a bill but misplaced it and paid it late. Neither issue seemed major at first, but the little patterns started forming cracks beneath the surface.

One Thursday evening, Ethan walked in late again to find Lily sitting at the table, staring at the dinner she had kept warm for over an hour. He apologized and said he simply lost track of time. She nodded but whispered, "I need to feel like I can depend on your words."

Her honesty stopped him. He realized trust was not broken in a single moment but in repeated disappointments. He reached for her hand and said, "I am sorry. You are right. I want my word to mean something to you."

That weekend, Lily found a note taped to the bathroom mirror: "I will be home by five today. I want you to trust me again." And he was. Not only that day, but the next, and the next. Slowly, consistency began stitching the loose threads back together.

By the end of that month, Lily told him, "I feel safe again."

Trust was rebuilt not through big gestures, but through steady faithfulness.

***

Proverbs 20:6 observes that many people claim to be faithful, but a truly trustworthy person is rare. Trust is not built by declarations but by consistent actions that match those declarations. Scripture paints trustworthiness as a mark of godly character.

Jesus taught the same principle in Luke 16:10, saying that those who are faithful in little will be faithful in much. In marriage, the "little" things often matter most: being on time, following through, speaking with honesty, keeping confidences, and showing up emotionally.

Colossians 3:9 reminds believers to "not lie to one another," because truthfulness forms the bedrock of every relationship. When spouses tell the truth consistently—about small things as well as big things—they create a foundation where love can rest securely.

These passages combined show that trust grows when character meets consistency.

***

Trust is not a single event but an ongoing pattern woven into daily life. When husbands and wives commit to consistency, they reflect the faithfulness God shows toward His people. Lamentations 3:23 describes God's mercies as new every morning, steady and predictable. That steady faithfulness fosters security. In marriage, consistency creates that same sense of safety.

Trust grows when spouses follow through on what they say, whether it is a small promise or a large commitment. Luke 16:10 reminds us that God notices faithfulness in the smallest details. When spouses pay attention to the small things—sending the text they said they would, being where they promised to be, speaking gently even when tired—they are building trust brick by brick.

Trust also grows through emotional consistency. A spouse who responds with kindness one day but sarcasm the next creates unpredictability. But when emotional steadiness becomes a habit, the home becomes a place of refuge rather than stress. Proverbs 3:3 encourages believers to bind love and faithfulness around their hearts. When a husband or wife does this, trust deepens naturally.

There will be seasons when one spouse falls short. Trust is not perfection. It is the commitment to repair quickly, apologize sincerely, and return to steady patterns of reliability. Healing takes time, but God honors humility and consistency.

A marriage rooted in trust becomes strong enough to withstand storms. The couple learns they can depend on one another. They know promises are not empty. They know love is not unstable. This deep security transforms the way they communicate, support each other, and walk through life together.

FROM HIS PERSPECTIVE

A few weeks ago, I was talking with a close friend who admitted something quietly. He said, "I want my wife to trust me deeply, but sometimes I give her reasons to hesitate." He explained how he often promised things with good intentions but did not follow through. "I never mean to break trust," he said, "but I can tell she watches to see if I will keep my word."

As he talked, I saw myself in parts of his story. Good intentions are not enough. What builds trust is reliability. I realized I want my wife to feel safe depending on me. When I say I will do something, I want my actions to affirm that she can count on me.

I have been practicing small changes—texting when I say I will, finishing tasks when I promise, listening when I said I would give her my full attention. The more consistent I am, the more I see her relax. She should not have to wonder whether I will follow through. Trust grows in moments where I show faithfulness steadily, not dramatically.

FROM HER PERSPECTIVE

There were seasons in my life when trust felt difficult, not because of my husband, but because of my past. I grew up in an environment where promises were often broken. People said one thing and did another. As a child, I learned to brace myself for disappointment.

When I got married, God began healing this slowly. Each time my husband followed through, each time he kept a promise, each time he spoke truth even when it was uncomfortable, something in my heart softened. Consistency has been one of the gentlest ways God has restored my sense of safety.

I am grateful for a marriage where trust keeps growing. It is not perfect, but it is honest. And each day we practice consistency, I feel more secure. Trust is built in layers, and with God's help, those layers grow deeper and stronger.

PRAYER

Lord, thank You for being perfectly faithful. Teach us to reflect Your steadiness in our marriage. Help us build trust through integrity, reliability, and humility. Strengthen the areas where we struggle, and fill our home with Your peace. Amen.

CONVERSATION PROMPTS

1. When it comes to trust, what actions or patterns from me make you feel safest and most secure? Are there small areas where consistency would make a meaningful difference in how you experience reliability and peace in our relationship?

2. Are there places in our marriage, big or small, where trust has been strained or where you still feel hesitation? How can we work together—with honesty, prayer, and gentle communication—to rebuild trust and restore full confidence?

CONNECTION PRACTICE

Each of you choose one small promise you can realistically keep today and follow through on it fully. Let it be simple but meaningful, a gentle reminder of reliability. At the end of the day, check in with one another by asking, "Did anything today make you feel supported or unsupported by me" Listen softly and without defensiveness. Affirm one small action you can take tomorrow to build steadiness and emotional safety together.

12. Gratitude as a Daily Practice

"In every thing give thanks: for this is
the will of God in Christ Jesus concerning you."
1 Thessalonians 5:18

During World War II, U.S. Army pilot Captain Eddie Rickenbacker and his crew were forced to ditch their plane into the Pacific Ocean after running out of fuel. For twenty-one days they floated on small rafts, battling exhaustion, hunger, dehydration, and sharks. Most men would have surrendered to despair. Instead, Rickenbacker insisted on one practice every single day: giving thanks.

Even when the sun scorched their skin, he led the crew in prayers of gratitude. Even when their food supply shrank to almost nothing, he encouraged the men to thank God for life, for each other, and for hope.

One afternoon, after a long time of prayer and thanksgiving, a seagull landed on Rickenbacker's head. The crew caught it and used it for food and fishing bait, which kept them alive until rescue. Rickenbacker always believed that the seagull came as a direct answer to sustained gratitude and prayer.

Afterward, he told reporters, "Gratitude kept us steady. It kept us alive."

His story shows a powerful truth: thanksgiving is not a reaction to comfort. It is a posture that carries us through both hardship and blessing.

***

1 Thessalonians 5:18 tells believers to "give thanks in all circumstances," not because every circumstance is pleasant, but because God is present in every circumstance. Gratitude opens the heart to see God's hand even in difficulty.

Philippians 4:6 teaches that thanksgiving is part of prayer itself. It shifts anxiety into trust, reminding us that God provides, protects, and guides. Gratitude strengthens faith by helping us see beyond the moment.

Colossians 3:15 adds that we are called to "be thankful." This is not accidental; it is an intentional act of the will. When couples practice gratitude toward God and toward each other, their marriage becomes warmer, steadier, and more joyful.

These Scriptures show that thanksgiving is not just a feeling. It is a daily practice that shapes how we see God, ourselves, and each other.

***

Gratitude is one of the simplest yet most transformative habits in marriage. When spouses regularly thank each other for small and big things, they cultivate a culture of appreciation rather than expectation.

Philippians 4:6 reminds us that gratitude changes the climate of the heart. It shifts focus from what frustrates to what blesses. Couples who regularly thank God for one another find it easier to extend grace, forgive quickly, and enjoy the daily moments that might otherwise go unnoticed.

Colossians 3:15 calls believers to let peace rule in their hearts, and gratitude often becomes the doorway through which peace enters. When a husband says, "Thank you for how you support our family," or when a wife says, "I appreciate the way you make me feel loved," it strengthens emotional intimacy.

Gratitude also counters resentment. It reminds both spouses that they are on the same team, each carrying weight in different ways. Even during seasons of stress, saying "I see your effort" or "I notice what you're doing" dissolves tension before it grows.

Scripture never treats gratitude as a background virtue. It is central to spiritual maturity and relational health. When practiced daily, thanksgiving becomes a gentle but powerful force that softens rough edges and binds hearts together.

A marriage filled with gratitude becomes a marriage filled with peace. It becomes a home where both spouses feel valued, noticed, and cherished.

FROM HIS PERSPECTIVE

A few days ago, I watched a friend of mine at work pack up his tools. He paused, looked at a photo of his wife on his desk, and said, "I realized something this morning. I complain way too much about the little things and forget to thank her for the hundred things she does without being asked."

He said it quietly, almost to himself. It hit me hard.

I started thinking about the moments I take for granted. The peaceful mornings Emeline creates. The meals she prepares. The way she manages our home with such commitment. Gratitude does not come naturally to me every day, but I am learning that when I practice it, our whole atmosphere changes.

When I thank her intentionally, her eyes soften. When I notice her efforts, her spirit seems lighter. Gratitude is not hard; it is simply a choice. And that choice brings warmth into our marriage every time I make it.

FROM HER PERSPECTIVE

I have learned that gratitude helps my heart stay soft. There are days when small frustrations try to grow bigger than they should, and in those moments, choosing to thank God for Emmett immediately shifts my perspective. It reminds me of his kindness, his effort, and the ways he loves our family.

Gratitude also helps me communicate better. When I say, "I appreciate you," it makes space for affection. It helps me focus on what is good rather than on what is missing. And the more I practice it, the more peaceful our home feels.

God has used gratitude to calm my anxious thoughts and to steady my emotions. It is a simple discipline, but it has brought so much beauty into our marriage.

PRAYER

Lord, teach us to cultivate hearts of gratitude. Help us notice the blessings You place in our daily lives and the gifts You have given us in each other. Shape our marriage into one marked by appreciation, joy, and peace. Amen.

CONVERSATION PROMPTS

1. What is something I do regularly that you are grateful for, but may not have

expressed recently? What small or unseen acts of love matter most to you, and how can we acknowledge them more openly in our daily life together?

2. When life feels stressful or overwhelming, what helps you remember to stay thankful? How can we remind each other gently to practice gratitude even when the season feels heavy, and what specific things can I do that help you feel appreciated?

CONNECTION PRACTICES

Each of you write down three specific things your spouse did this week that made a difference, even the small and easily overlooked acts. Share them aloud with sincerity, letting gratitude soften and strengthen your connection. Before bed, take a moment to name one thing your spouse did today that you genuinely appreciated. Keep it simple and heartfelt. These small expressions of thanks create warmth, recognition, and a deeper sense of being valued.

13. Serving Each Other with Joy

"For even the Son of man came not to be ministered unto,
but to minister, and to give his life a ransom for many."
Mark 10:45

During the later years of his life, President Jimmy Carter volunteered with Habitat for Humanity, not occasionally but consistently, even into his nineties. One year, shortly after undergoing brain surgery and recovering from a severe fall, Carter showed up to a build site wearing a bandage over his eye and using a cane for balance.

A reporter asked him, "Why come out here when you could rest? No one would expect you to be doing physical labor at your age."

Carter smiled and said simply, "Because serving people makes me feel alive. This is what love looks like."

He spent the entire day hammering, sawing, painting, and encouraging the volunteers around him. People said he would often take the tasks no one else wanted—not because they were easy, but because they helped someone else feel supported.

His example shows something deeply biblical. Joy does not come from comfort. It comes from choosing to serve with a willing and humble heart.

***

Serving each other within marriage looks simple on the surface—doing chores, helping with tasks, offering support—but the heart behind serving is what gives it spiritual meaning. Some days service feels effortless, and other days it feels costly. Joyful service comes from remembering why we serve: not to earn appreciation, but to express love.

This kind of service begins in small, daily choices. Bringing a cup of tea without being asked. Taking over a responsibility when the other is tired. Stepping in with kindness instead of waiting to be noticed. These moments quietly shape the emotional climate of the home.

Halfway through this call to serve, Scripture offers a powerful reminder. Mark 10:45 says that Jesus came "not to be served, but to serve," giving us a model not of duty, but of willing sacrifice. His example shifts our perspective. Serving each other becomes an act of worship, a reflection of the heart of Christ, not just a task list.

When spouses embrace this mindset, service becomes meaningful rather than burdensome. It becomes a way of saying, "Your well-being matters to me," and "We are in this together." And in that mutual offering, joy rises.

***

Serving each other with joy strengthens the foundation of marriage. It turns daily life into a shared mission rather than a divided workload. When one spouse steps in with generosity, the other feels valued and supported. Over time, this creates a rhythm of kindness that blesses both hearts.

Galatians 5:13 teaches believers to "serve one another humbly in love." When applied to marriage, this means choosing generosity even when tired, helping even when unnoticed, and giving without keeping score. Joyful service is not about perfection but about intentionality.

Proverbs 11:25 says that "whoever refreshes others will be refreshed." Serving with a joyful spirit ends up blessing the one who gives. It lifts heaviness. It strengthens intimacy. It turns the home into a place marked by grace rather than resentment.

Joyful service does not mean neglecting your own needs. Healthy service includes communication, mutual respect, and shared responsibility. It means asking, "How can I lighten your load today?" just as honestly as you ask, "Can you help me with mine?"

Over time, serving with joy creates a home where tenderness comes naturally, where both spouses feel cared for, and where the heart of Christ is reflected in daily rhythms.

FROM HIS PERSPECTIVE

Last month I watched one of my close friends at a family gathering. His wife had been recovering from a back injury, and I noticed how quietly he served her. He carried her plate, helped her stand, and checked on her every few minutes—not in a smothering way, but with genuine tenderness.

At one point, she whispered, "Thank you," and he said, "It is joy for me." And he meant it.

Driving home that evening, I thought about what it means for me to serve my own wife with that kind of heart. Not out of duty. Not out of obligation. But because loving her well is one of the greatest privileges I have.

The more I practice serving with joy, the more connected I feel to Emeline. It does not have to be dramatic. Sometimes it is folding laundry. Sometimes it is listening when she needs to talk. Sometimes it is taking the task she least wants to do.

Serving her with joy is one of the clearest ways I can reflect Christ in our home.

FROM HER PERSPECTIVE

I am learning that joyful service begins with seeing my marriage as a partnership, not a competition. When I serve Emmett with love, even in small ways, something gentle happens inside me. My heart softens. My patience grows. And I feel more connected to him.

There are days when serving feels easy and days when it feels like one more responsibility. In those moments, I remind myself that God sees every act of love, even the ones no one notices. Serving with joy is not about pretending to be cheerful. It is about choosing kindness, even when the day feels heavy.

I am grateful for a marriage where we are learning to serve each other more naturally. It reminds me that love grows best through ordinary acts of care.

PRAYER

Lord, teach us to serve each other with joy, humility, and love. Help us follow the example of Christ, who served willingly and generously. Strengthen our hearts to give without grumbling, to support without hesitation, and to love through our actions as well as our words. Amen.

CONVERSATION PROMPTS

1. What types of service make you feel most noticed, supported, and valued in our home? Are there specific daily or weekly actions that help you feel deeply loved, and how can we prioritize those intentionally?

2. Are there moments when you feel tempted to keep mental score of who is doing more or carrying more? How can we gently talk about those feelings, rebalance responsibilities, and return to a place of joyful partnership instead of quiet resentment?

CONNECTION PRACTICES

Choose one task you normally handle and swap it with your spouse for the day, not to measure effort but to bless one another with gratitude and understanding. At some point, pause and ask, "What can I do right now to lighten your load" Then follow through with genuine joy. These simple acts of shared support create warmth, appreciation, and a deeper sense of partnership as you carry life together with kindness.

14: Protecting Your Marriage from Distractions

"Keep thy heart with all diligence;
for out of it are the issues of life."
Proverbs 4:23

A few years ago, the family had a close friend named Marcus. He was the kind of person who made everyone feel welcomed the moment he walked into a room. His marriage had once been strong, held together by deep affection and years of shared memories. But little by little, distractions began to slip in unnoticed.

It started harmlessly. Marcus poured himself into new hobbies, late-night work projects, and constant phone scrolling. His wife, Hannah, would occasionally ask if they could spend more time together, and he always responded with a quick, "Soon, I promise." He meant well, but the days kept filling up with everything except connection.

Over time, the small gaps in their relationship widened into quiet distance. Hannah still smiled at gatherings, but her eyes carried a tiredness that was easy to miss. Marcus still talked about how much he loved his family, but he rarely slowed down long enough to show it. Their marriage did not break suddenly. It simply faded under the weight of everything that seemed urgent but wasn't truly important.

One evening, after a difficult season neither of them had words for, Marcus sat on the edge of our couch and said quietly, "I thought I had more time. I thought these things could wait." His voice trembled. "I did not realize how far apart we had grown."

***

Distractions often enter the marriage long before anyone notices them. They arrive disguised as responsibilities, opportunities, small escapes, or simple habits. None of these things are wrong on their own. Life is full of commitments and interests. But when the good begins to quietly overshadow the essential, connection fades.

Many couples do not drift because of conflict, but because of crowded schedules, exhaustion, or constant digital noise. Hearts begin to live parallel lives instead of shared ones. At first it feels like nothing has changed. Then one day either spouse realizes they have not had a meaningful conversation in weeks.

Guarding the heart involves guarding what enters it and what pulls it away. It means paying attention to what steals time, drains energy, or numbs affection. It requires intentional awareness so that the most important relationship in your home stays protected. When couples guard their hearts together, they shield their marriage from slow erosion.

***

Protecting the marriage from distractions is part of spiritual stewardship. God designed marriage as a covenant, a place where love is nurtured through intentional attention. When distractions rule our days, they quietly weaken connection. Protecting the marriage means creating boundaries around what matters most.

Jesus taught in Luke 21:34 to "be careful" that our hearts are not weighed down by the busyness of life. The warning was not only spiritual, but relational. A heart filled with noise cannot recognize the needs of the person right beside it.

Protecting your marriage does not require eliminating every interest or responsibility. It means knowing which voices to turn down and which voices to prioritize. It means putting the phone away when your spouse speaks. It means saying no to unnecessary commitments when your schedule is already strained. It means choosing rest when exhaustion threatens closeness.

Ephesians 5:15 calls believers to "walk wisely." A wise marriage pays attention to drift early, not after distance grows painful. It pays attention to tone, timing, and tenderness. It notices when conversation decreases or affection grows thin. Protection begins in these small observations.

A protected marriage is not rigid—it is mindful. It makes room for joy, conversation, shared rest, and spiritual connection. It guards intimacy by guarding time. It refuses to let the urgent overshadow the meaningful. When couples protect their marriage from distractions, they create a place where love can breathe and flourish.

***

FROM HIS PERSPECTIVE

A while ago, I had a conversation with a friend who admitted he barely talked to his wife during the week. "I am home every night," he said, "but I am not really present." He described how work emails, sports highlights, and online browsing kept him mentally somewhere else long after he walked through the front door.

He said something that stuck with me: "I did not realize distraction was becoming neglect."

I thought about our home. I thought about the quiet moments when my wife needed my attention, but I was half listening with my eyes on a screen. I am learning that protecting my marriage requires protecting my focus. When I look at her fully, when I give her my presence, I see her heart in ways I would have missed otherwise.

I want my marriage to be strengthened by my attention, not weakened by distraction. Being fully present is one of the clearest ways I can show love.

FROM HER PERSPECTIVE

I have noticed that distraction shows up most when my heart is tired. I start scrolling through my phone or filling my schedule because it feels easier than slowing down. But when I do that too often, I begin to feel distant from my husband without meaning to be.

Protecting our marriage means noticing when I am drifting emotionally. It means choosing conversation instead of silence, choosing eye contact instead of multitasking, choosing to share my heart rather than burying it under busy thoughts.

There is so much peace in knowing that when I turn my attention toward my husband, I am turning it toward something God treasures. Our marriage grows strongest when we guard it from the things that so easily steal our focus.

PRAYER

Lord, help us guard our marriage from distractions that weaken connection. Teach us to be present, attentive, and wise. Protect our hearts from drift and remind us to prioritize each other with intention and love. Strengthen our bond as we honor You in how we give our time and attention. Amen.

CONVERSATION PROMPTS

1. What are the biggest distractions pulling at your attention lately? How do they affect the way you feel connected or disconnected from me? What practical steps could we take together to reduce their impact and keep our relationship centered?

2. When do you feel the most noticed, valued, and prioritized by me? Are there specific times of day or small habits that help you feel emotionally close, and how can we build more of those moments into our routine?

CONNECTION PRACTICES

Sit together for ten quiet, uninterrupted minutes with no phone, no television, and no multitasking. Simply talk, breathe, and reconnect without pressure. Afterward, each of you choose one distraction to lay down or reduce over the next seven days. Share your choices openly, then pray for grace and steadiness to follow through. Let this become a gentle reset that clears space for presence, attention, and a deeper sense of closeness throughout the week.

15. Renewing the Mind Together

"And be not conformed to this world: but be ye transformed
by the renewing of your mind, that ye may prove |
what is that good, and acceptable, and perfect, will of God."
Romans 12:2

One of the most remarkable true stories from the medieval church involves Bernard of Clairvaux, the twelfth-century monk whose writings shaped Christian thought for generations. Bernard was known for his passionate pursuit of God, but what history often forgets is the reason behind it. Before he became a spiritual leader, Bernard went through a season when he was deeply troubled in mind and heart. He was overwhelmed by uncertainty, plagued with internal battles, and unsure of his purpose.

During that time, Bernard's older brother, Guy, saw what was happening. Instead of criticizing him or telling him to "snap out of it," Guy began gently encouraging Bernard to turn his thoughts toward Scripture, prayer, and the hope found in Christ. He prayed with him, walked with him, spoke life over him, and reminded him of God's promises day after day.

History records that Bernard later said he might never have pursued God so deeply if his brother had not helped "lift his mind out of the shadows." Guy's gentle influence became the very spark that led Bernard into the life of devotion he is now famous for.

Their story reminds us of something powerful within marriage. Sometimes one spouse helps the other lift their mind back toward truth. Sometimes one heart needs the other to help pull it out of the shadows. Renewing the mind is not meant to be a solo journey. It can become a shared rhythm that strengthens the whole home.

***

Thoughts shape emotions, relationships, and the atmosphere of a home far more than most couples realize. A discouraged mind makes everything feel heavier. A fearful mind shrinks hope. A distracted mind weakens connection. Renewing the mind means becoming intentional about what fills it, and how it influences the heart.

This is where Scripture's wisdom becomes practical. Halfway into Paul's instruction, Romans 12:2 invites believers to be transformed through "the renewing of your mind." Renewal does not happen instantly. It grows through repeated choices—what we meditate on, what we rehearse within ourselves, and what we invite into our thoughts.

When spouses encourage each other toward godly thinking, they become a source of strength, not strain. They help each other recognize lies, fears, or discouragement, and gently point the heart back to truth.

***

Renewing the mind together is one of the most powerful ways a couple can grow spiritually. When two people influence each other's thoughts with grace and Scripture, they build a foundation of emotional resilience. Paul teaches in Philippians 4:8 to think on "whatever is true, noble, right, pure, lovely, admirable." When a spouse helps the other focus on these things, the atmosphere of the marriage becomes lighter and more peaceful.

Renewing the mind is not about ignoring pain or pretending everything is fine. It is about choosing what to dwell on. It means replacing self-doubt with God's truth, replacing anxiety with prayer, replacing frustration with perspective, and replacing negative assumptions with compassion.

Couples can practice this by praying Scripture over each other, sharing encouraging verses, speaking life-giving words, or gently redirecting thoughts when negativity begins to spiral. Hebrews 10:24 says to "spur one another on toward love and good deeds." In marriage, this often looks like helping each other remember God's goodness when circumstances feel overwhelming.

The mind is a garden. If left unattended, weeds grow quickly. But when tended with care—through Scripture, prayer, conversation, and gratitude—it becomes a place where peace flourishes. Renewing the mind as a couple strengthens not only spiritual life, but emotional well-being and relational intimacy.

FROM HIS PERSPECTIVE

A friend of mine told me recently that he often struggles with negative thoughts. He said, "I can ruin a whole day in my head before breakfast." His wife noticed this pattern and began leaving small handwritten verses near his keys, in his lunchbox, or tucked into the dashboard of his car.

He told me, "Those notes helped me redirect my thoughts more than she realized." Over time, he began speaking truth back to himself: "God is with me. This worry will not control me. I am not failing, just learning." His entire outlook changed, and he said his marriage grew stronger because of it.

Hearing his story made me realize how important it is to speak life into my own wife's mind when her thoughts grow heavy. When I remind her of truth, when I pray over her, when I help her see God's goodness in hard seasons, I become part of her renewal—not her pressure.

Renewing the mind is something we can do side by side. And as we do it, I see hope return more easily in both of us.

FROM HER PERSPECTIVE

I am learning that my thoughts influence the tone of my entire day. When my mind gets caught in worry or discouragement, I can feel it affecting my attitude, my energy, and even the way I relate to my husband. But when I slow down and let God renew my mind, everything feels lighter.

Renewing my mind often begins with something simple—reading Scripture, speaking truth out loud, or asking my husband to pray for me when I feel overwhelmed. Those moments help me redirect my thoughts away from fear and toward faith.

I am grateful that my husband and I can remind each other of God's promises. When he speaks gently into my doubts or prays over my stress, it strengthens me in ways he may not fully realize. Renewing the mind together has become a way we strengthen our marriage and draw closer to God.

PRAYER

Lord, help us renew our minds daily through Your Word. Teach us to encourage each other toward truth, hope, and peace. Guard our thoughts from discouragement and fill our home with the goodness of Your promises. Transform us from the inside out as we walk with You together. Amen.

CONVERSATION PROMPTS

1. What kinds of encouragement help you most when your thoughts feel heavy or overwhelmed? Are there words, Scriptures, or gentle reminders that make a real difference for you, and how can I offer them more intentionally?

2. Are there recurring thought patterns—fear, self-criticism, worry, overthinking—that weigh you down more than others? How can we help each other gently redirect those patterns toward truth without sounding dismissive or impatient?

CONNECTION PRACTICES

Each of you choose one Scripture that has encouraged you recently and share it with your spouse. Explain gently why it helped you and how you hope to carry it into the week ahead. Then sit together for sixty quiet seconds, asking God silently to renew your spouse's mind. When the minute ends, speak one simple sentence of blessing over each other. Let this exchange become a moment of spiritual closeness and refreshment.

16. Weathering Financial Stress

"But my God shall supply all your need
according to his riches in glory by Christ Jesus."
Philippians 4:19

When our son Paldy was born, we stepped into one of the hardest seasons of our early marriage. Medical bills piled higher every week. The car needed repairs we had no idea how to pay for. Our pantry looked smaller than ever, and we stretched a week of groceries into something that lasted almost two. Every dollar mattered. Every surprise expense felt like a jolt we were not ready for.

I remember one night clearly. The baby was finally asleep, and we sat at the kitchen table surrounded by papers, envelopes, an old calculator, and two very tired parents. I stared at the numbers and whispered, "I do not know how this is going to work." My spouse rubbed his forehead, trying to hide the worry in his eyes, and I knew he feared letting us down even though he did not say it out loud.

We sat in silence for a long time. Then I reached for his hand and said, "We are in this together. Whatever happens, we will face it side by side." Something shifted in that moment. The bills did not disappear, but the pressure loosened just enough for us to breathe again.

That month taught us more about partnership than any book or seminar ever could. We learned how to pray over our bank statements, how to laugh when our budget felt impossibly tight, and how to say "thank You" for small provisions that showed up at exactly the right time. Most of all, we discovered that financial stress can pull a couple apart or draw them closer, depending on how they choose to walk through it..

***

Financial stress can create a heaviness that few other pressures match. It affects sleep, emotions, decisions, and even the way couples speak to each other. Bills have a way of stirring fear. Budgets can strain communication. But financial challenge is not a sign of failure—it is a normal part of life that requires unity.

What matters is how two spouses handle the weight together. Some couples drift into blame. Others retreat into silence. Unity is not automatic; it is cultivated intentionally through shared decisions, gentle communication, and honesty about what feels overwhelming.

Halfway through this truth, Philippians 4:19 reminds us that "God will supply all your needs according to His riches." Not all wants. Not all timelines. But every true need. This verse does not erase the budgeting or the hard conversations, but it anchors them. It keeps the heart steady when the numbers feel tight and the future feels uncertain.

When couples cling to God together in financial seasons, they discover peace that does not come from their bank account—it comes from trusting God's faithfulness. Stress becomes bearable because they carry it as one.

***

Weathering financial stress as a couple is about far more than bills and numbers. It is about protecting unity. Money pressure can either weaken a marriage or strengthen it depending on the posture of the spouses.

Proverbs 21:5 reminds us that wise planning brings stability. When couples communicate honestly, create realistic budgets, and make decisions with unity, they reduce unnecessary tension. But wisdom works best when grace accompanies it. Sometimes unexpected expenses come, income fluctuates, or emergencies arise. In those moments, grace must fill the spaces where control disappears.

Financial unity grows when couples share their fears instead of hiding them. When they pray together over their needs. When they ask God for wisdom rather than carrying the burden alone. Jesus taught in Matthew 6:33 to seek God first—financial peace is often tied to spiritual focus.

A marriage becomes stronger when both spouses listen without judgment, support each other's concerns, and avoid comparing their situation to others. The enemy of financial unity is not poverty—it is isolation. When couples stand together, even lean months cannot uproot them.

Weathering financial stress with faith teaches patience, strengthens communication, and deepens trust. It prepares the marriage for future seasons with steadier hearts.

FROM HIS PERSPECTIVE

A friend of mine once told me how he used to hide financial stress from his wife. He thought shielding her from the worry was an act of love. But one day, during a particularly tight month, she found him in the garage staring at a stack of unpaid bills. His shoulders were slumped, and he looked defeated.

She walked over, put her hand on his back, and said, "Let me carry this with you." He told me he cried right there—not because of the bills, but because he realized he didn't have to bear the pressure alone.

That conversation changed their marriage. They started budgeting together, praying together, and facing decisions as one. Hearing his story helped me understand something important: I cannot protect my wife by hiding the hard things. I protect our unity by facing them with her, side by side.

FROM HER PERSPECTIVE

Financial stress affects my emotions more than I want to admit. I start imagining worst-case scenarios or feeling guilty for every expense, even small ones. When money feels tight, my heart can tighten too.

But I have learned that unity makes all the difference. When we talk about the numbers openly, when I feel heard instead of dismissed, and when we pray over our needs together, I feel peace settle into me again. I do not want solutions as much as I want partnership.

Financial seasons come and go, but what stays consistent is our choice to walk through them as a team. That unity means more to me than any number on a bank statement.

PRAYER

Lord, help us walk through financial stress with unity, wisdom, and peace. Guard our hearts from fear and frustration. Teach us to trust You with every need and to support each other with gentleness and patience. Strengthen our marriage as we face these challenges together. Amen.

CONVERSATION PROMPTS

1. When financial pressure rises, what emotions come up for you—fear, guilt, frustration, insecurity? How can I support you more gently in those moments so you feel safe and understood instead of overwhelmed or alone?

2. Are there areas of our finances—budgeting, saving, spending, future planning—where you feel disconnected from me or unsure about how we make decisions? What steps can we take to walk in closer unity and clearer communication?

CONNECTION PRACTICES

Sit together for five quiet minutes with your budget or bills in front of you. Pray calmly over each item, asking God for wisdom, provision, and unity, then thank Him for one specific way He has provided in the past. After praying, each of you suggest one small and realistic financial habit you would like to improve. Choose one to practice together this week, supporting each other gently as you build steadiness and shared responsibility.

17. Healing After Hurts

"He healeth the broken in heart, and bindeth up their wounds."
Psalm 147:3

One of the most moving accounts of relational healing in Scripture is the story of Joseph and his brothers. Years earlier, they had betrayed him in the most painful way imaginable. They sold him into slavery, lied to their father, and carried on with life as if Joseph's suffering didn't matter. The wounds they caused were deep, and Joseph lived with the consequences for years.

But when famine brought his brothers to Egypt seeking food, Joseph faced a moment none of them expected. He recognized them instantly. They did not recognize him. He could have chosen anger. He could have confronted them with fury or used his authority to repay the pain they caused. Instead, Joseph stepped out of the shadows and wept.

His tears were not weakness—they were the evidence of a heart willing to heal.

Joseph reassured them, saying, "Do not be afraid." In one breath, he released years of hurt and offered forgiveness that reached down to the roots of their betrayal. Genesis records that he "kissed all his brothers and wept over them," and they were reconciled.

Joseph's story reminds us that healing after hurt is not about pretending nothing happened. It is about choosing mercy over bitterness, compassion over resentment, and restoration over revenge. Healing is holy work—and in marriage, it becomes one of the most sacred journeys two hearts can walk together.

***

Hurts between spouses can run deep. Sometimes they come from sharp words spoken in frustration. Sometimes from misunderstandings, disappointments, or seasons of emotional distance. Whatever the cause, pain inside a marriage can create emotional walls that feel impossible to climb.

Healing begins with honesty—honesty about the wound, honesty about feelings, and honesty about the desire to rebuild. Healing does not erase the past, but it allows the heart to move forward without carrying the weight of unspoken pain.

Halfway into this gentle work, Psalm 147:3 offers a truth that anchors the process: "He heals the brokenhearted and binds up their wounds." God does not ignore emotional pain. He moves toward it with tenderness. His healing does not rush or force. It restores patiently, one layer at a time.

When spouses invite God into their hurts, healing becomes possible even when emotions run deep. His presence softens defensiveness, quiets fear, and strengthens the desire to reconcile. Healing is not about winning—it is about restoring unity.

***

Healing after hurts requires humility, patience, and compassion. It asks both spouses to listen with empathy, speak with honesty, and offer grace even when it feels costly.

Ephesians 4:32 encourages believers to be "kind and compassionate to one another, forgiving each other, just as in Christ God forgave you." Kindness opens the door for vulnerable conversation. Compassion softens defensiveness. Forgiveness releases bitterness so reconciliation can grow.

Healing also involves responsibility. The spouse who caused the hurt must be willing to acknowledge the pain without excuses. The spouse who was hurt must be willing to share their feelings without attacking. Healing happens in the gentle space where honesty meets humility.

Colossians 3:13 reminds believers to bear with one another and forgive as the Lord forgave them. Forgiveness is not minimizing the wound—it is choosing not to let the wound rule the relationship. It is releasing the weight that keeps hearts distant.

Healthy healing includes time. Some hurts mend quickly. Others heal slowly. What matters is that both spouses walk the journey together, with patience, prayer, and a shared desire for closeness.

When healing is pursued with love, marriages grow stronger than before. Scars may remain, but they become reminders of God's mercy, not of lingering pain.

FROM HIS PERSPECTIVE

Not long ago, I had a moment with Emeline when I realized I had hurt her without meaning to. I had dismissed a concern she shared because I thought I had a better perspective. Later that night, I noticed she was quiet, not in anger but in sadness.

When I asked what was wrong, she hesitated. Then she said, "I needed you to hear my heart, not fix the situation." Her words pierced me. I realized I had wounded her with carelessness, not malice.

I apologized—not with quick words, but with intention. I told her I understood why it hurt, and I meant it. That moment became a turning point for me. I saw how much healing happens when a husband listens deeply and takes responsibility. Her hurt became a place for my growth, and our marriage felt more connected afterward.

Healing begins when I lower my defenses and open my heart. It changes everything.

FROM HER PERSPECTIVE

Healing after hurt has been one of the most sacred parts of our marriage. It is never easy to say, "That really hurt me," but every time I do, and Emmett (usually!) responds with compassion rather than defensiveness, something inside me relaxes.

Healing does not mean forgetting. It means releasing the grip of pain so love can flow again. It means choosing to trust that my heart is safe with him, even when I feel vulnerable.

God has taught me that healing happens in layers. Sometimes quickly, sometimes slowly. What matters most is walking the journey together with honesty, gentleness, and prayer. I have learned that when we invite God into our hurts, He brings restoration that feels deeper than the pain that came before.

PRAYER

Lord, heal the tender places in our marriage. Help us speak honestly, listen with compassion, and forgive with Your grace. Bind our wounds and draw our hearts closer than before. Teach us to walk in humility, patience, and love as You restore what pain has touched. Amen.

CONVERSATION PROMPTS

1. Is there a wound—big or small—that still feels tender between us? What emotion sits beneath it… sadness, fear, embarrassment, or disappointment? How can we talk about it gently so healing can begin instead of the pain remaining unspoken?

2. When you are hurt, what makes you feel comforted and safe—time, reassurance, prayer, physical closeness, space to process? How can we create a healing environment for each other, especially during vulnerable moments?

CONNECTION PRACTICES

Take a quiet moment for one spouse to share a small hurt from the past month. The other repeats back what they heard, not to defend, but to understand. Close with a soft word of reassurance. Afterward, each of you choose one simple act of repair, such as a note, a gentle touch, or a warm affirmation that communicates, "I want closeness." These small, humble steps rebuild trust in deep and lasting ways.

18. Cultivating Spiritual Rhythms

"And they continued stedfastly in the apostles' doctrine and fellowship,

and in breaking of bread, and in prayers.."

Acts 2:42

One of the most beautiful true accounts of shared spiritual rhythm comes from the life of Susanna Wesley, the mother of John and Charles Wesley. Though she lived in the early 1700s and raised nineteen children, history remembers her not simply as a mother, but as a woman whose spiritual habits quietly shaped an entire movement.

Susanna's daily life was chaotic. Her home was filled with noise, chores, teaching, and constant interruptions. Yet she cultivated a rhythm that never wavered. Every day, she set aside a specific time to pray and read Scripture—even when it felt impossible. When there was no quiet place left in the house, she would sit in her chair, pull her apron over her head, and create a small sanctuary beneath that simple cloth. Her children knew: "Mother is praying."

But the part often forgotten is how Susanna shared these rhythms with her husband, Samuel. Their marriage saw hardship, financial stress, separations due to Samuel's work, and deep grief from losing several children. Yet throughout it all, they prayed together, sang hymns together, and read Scripture as a couple. Those rhythms steadied their love and strengthened their unity.

Their sons eventually led a revival that touched continents, but it began in a home where husband and wife walked with God side by side, quietly and faithfully.

Susanna's story reminds us that spiritual rhythms do not have to look dramatic. They only have to be shared. Small moments of spiritual unity can anchor a marriage through any season.

***

Spiritual rhythms in marriage begin with daily decisions shaped by intention rather than emotion. A couple does not grow spiritually by accident. Growth happens through repeated, simple habits—praying together, reading Scripture, pausing to thank God, worshipping on hard days and easy days, and pointing each other toward Christ.

The goal is not perfection or routine for routine's sake. Spiritual rhythms strengthen emotional intimacy, deepen peace, and create a shared foundation for decision-making and conflict resolution. When couples pursue God together, their hearts move closer not only to Him but to each other.

Halfway into this truth, Acts 2:42 gives a clear picture of early believers: they "devoted themselves to the apostles' teaching, to fellowship, to the breaking of bread, and to prayer." Devotion—not convenience—was the heartbeat of their rhythm. And devotion is what anchors couples today. When a husband and wife choose to pause long enough to pray or open Scripture, they invite God into the center of their marriage.

Those small choices begin to transform the home from the inside out.

***

Cultivating spiritual rhythms as a couple brings stability into a world filled with noise and uncertainty. When spouses pursue God together, they remind each other of hope on discouraging days and truth in confusing seasons. Their faith becomes intertwined, forming a bond that withstands pressure.

Deuteronomy 6:6–7 speaks of keeping God's words close to the heart and discussing them "when you sit at home and when you walk along the road." Shared spiritual rhythms are simply that—woven into conversations, bedtime routines, and everyday life.

Not every rhythm will look the same. Some couples thrive with morning prayer. Others connect through nightly devotion. Some share worship on car rides or pray during stressful moments. The form is flexible; the consistency is what matters.

Spiritual rhythms also help couples discern God's direction. When decisions arise—parenting choices, financial steps, relational conflicts—couples who pray together find clarity more quickly. Their hearts are aligned around the same truth. Their spirits become more receptive to guidance.

Spiritual rhythms do not erase hardship. But they strengthen the marriage for whatever may come. Two hearts kneeling together rise stronger than they were before.

FROM HIS PERSPECTIVE

A few months ago, I had a conversation with a friend who said something simple that stuck with me. He told me, "My marriage changed when my wife and I started praying together again." He said it wasn't dramatic. They didn't pray long prayers or read chapters of Scripture every night. They simply held hands for a minute or two and invited God into their day.

He told me, "I thought prayer had to be perfect. It doesn't. It just has to be shared."

That conversation reminded me how powerful small spiritual rhythms really are. When I pray with my wife, even for a moment, something inside me settles. We feel like we are fighting our battles together, not separately. My heart softens toward her. My worries lose their grip. And the presence of God fills the quiet space between us.

Cultivating spiritual rhythms together is not about effort. It is about connection. And every time we pursue God side by side, our marriage grows deeper and stronger.

FROM HER PERSPECTIVE

I am learning that spiritual rhythms do not have to be complicated to be meaningful. Sometimes it is reading a verse together before bed. Sometimes it is a quick prayer in the car before facing a stressful day. Sometimes it is sharing what God whispered into my heart that morning.

These moments keep me grounded. They remind me that I am not pursuing God alone. Walking with my husband spiritually draws us closer, even when life feels busy. When we pray together, I feel steadier. When we read Scripture together, I feel connected not only to God but to him.

I cherish these rhythms because they remind me that we are building something eternal, not just practical. We are cultivating a spiritual home.

PRAYER

Lord, teach us to pursue You together with unity and devotion. Help us build spiritual rhythms that strengthen our marriage, steady our hearts, and draw us closer to Your truth. Let our shared faith become a source of peace, direction, and deep connection. Amen.

CONVERSATION PROMPTS

1. What spiritual habits make you feel closest to God, and which of those would you like to share with me? Are there practices—prayer, Scripture reading, worship—that help you feel spiritually supported in our marriage?

2. Are there any barriers that make it difficult for us to pray or pursue spiritual habits together—discomfort, busyness, insecurity, past experiences? How can we gently overcome those barriers and create rhythms that feel natural and comforting?

CONNECTION PRACTICES

Choose one simple spiritual rhythm to practice together for just three minutes today. It may be a short prayer, reading a single verse aloud, or thanking God for one blessing. Keep it gentle and joyful. Then pick one Scripture to display somewhere visible in your home this week, whether by the bed, on the fridge, or near the door. Let it quietly shape your thoughts, soften your conversations, and deepen your shared pursuit of God.

19. Practicing Patience in Daily Life

"But let patience have her perfect work,
that ye may be perfect and entire, wanting nothing."
James 1:4

The night was unnervingly still. Beyond the hills of Sinai, the wind whispered across the desert floor, carrying sand that hissed against cloaks and tents. The people gathered in uneasy clusters, glancing at the mountain that stood like a dark silhouette against the sky. They waited. And the longer they waited, the more fear seeped into frustration.

Moses had been gone far too many days.

At first their hope sounded steady: "He will return." "God is with him." But as time dragged on, daylight thinned their confidence and nightfall chilled it. The desert felt louder and harsher, and under the weight of uncertainty, panic simmered.

Then someone cried out, "We need a god we can see."

That spark ignited a wildfire of restlessness. The people rushed to Aaron, their impatience pushing them toward choices they would later grieve. Their unsettled hearts tried to fill the silence with something—anything—that felt certain. Out of that impatience came one of Israel's most devastating moments: the golden calf.

The story reveals that impatience is never harmless. It leads to decisions shaped by fear rather than faith. Waiting well is spiritual strength. And in marriage, patience becomes a quiet protection that guards love from needless wounds.

***

Patience is often tested not in dramatic events but in the quiet moments of daily life—when plans change, when misunderstandings arise, when exhaustion pushes emotions to the surface, or when small irritations feel bigger than they should. Impatience usually grows when our expectations collide with reality.

Practicing patience requires slowing down long enough to breathe, notice what we feel, and respond with wisdom rather than reaction. It requires understanding that our spouse is not our opponent, but our companion—and that their pace, personality, or emotional rhythm is not meant to frustrate us, but to complement us.

Halfway through this truth, James 1:4 reminds us that patience—perseverance—must "finish its work," because it develops maturity and completeness. In other words, patience is not passive; it is shaping us. It is forming character. It is strengthening the foundation of our hearts and our relationships.

When couples learn to pause before reacting, listen before assuming, and speak gently instead of sharply, they create a home where peace grows naturally.

***

Practicing patience in marriage is one of the most powerful ways to build emotional safety. Patience lowers the temperature of conflict. It gives both spouses room to be human—room to make mistakes, to be tired, to need time, to learn and grow. Proverbs 14:29 teaches that patience brings understanding, while impatience leads to foolish decisions. This wisdom applies deeply to married life.

Patience is not about suppressing emotions. It is about managing them with love. It means saying, "Let me understand before I respond." It means offering grace on stressful days and choosing calm words instead of sharp ones.

Ephesians 4:2 encourages believers to be "completely humble and gentle; be patient, bearing with one another in love." Bearing with one another does not mean tolerating irritation. It means recognizing that both husband and wife are works in progress and extending kindness accordingly.

Patience grows through practice—small pauses, slower speech, thoughtful responses. The more it is practiced, the more natural it becomes. As couples choose patience consistently, their home becomes a sanctuary of peace rather than tension.

FROM HIS PERSPECTIVE

A few weeks ago, I watched a husband in our church lobby kneeling beside his son, helping him tie a stubborn shoelace while the boy grew increasingly frustrated. The father stayed calm, gently saying, "Try again. I'm right here." He repeated the same words over and over with a steady voice.

When they finally walked away, a friend whispered to me, "That man has the patience of a saint." But what struck me most was the joy on the father's face—not irritation, not frustration, but joy.

Driving home that day, I asked myself whether Emeline feels that same steadiness from me. Do I practice that quiet patience with her in our everyday moments? Do I slow down long enough to listen, to understand, to offer gentleness instead of urgency? Watching that father reminded me that patience is not weakness—it is strength held steady with love.

Marriage gives me daily opportunities to practice that kind of strength.

FROM HER PERSPECTIVE

I am learning that patience begins inside my thoughts long before it shows up in my words. When I feel overwhelmed or irritated, my mind starts racing ahead of my heart, and I can react more sharply than I mean to. But when I pause—even for a moment—I can choose grace instead of frustration.

Practicing patience has helped me see my husband's intentions more clearly. It reminds me that he is doing his best, even on days when we misunderstand each other. Patience softens my reactions, helps me listen better, and gives us space to reconnect when we drift.

I want our marriage to be a place where grace slows us down, not where impatience speeds us apart. With God's help, patience becomes a gift I can offer every day.

PRAYER

Lord, teach us to walk in patience. Help us slow down, listen with calmness, and respond with gentleness. Guard our hearts from reacting in frustration. Shape us into people who reflect Your love in the way we wait, speak, and care for one another. Amen.

CONVERSATION PROMPTS

1. In our everyday life together, what situations test your patience the most—tiredness, stress, interruptions, misunderstandings? How can I support you in those moments so you feel understood rather than pressured?

2. When you feel yourself becoming impatient, what helps you slow down and regain calm? Are there specific phrases, habits, or reminders that help you choose gentleness, and how can we practice them together?

CONNECTION PRACTICES

For one day, both of you practice pausing for three quiet seconds before responding in moments of tension or irritation. Use that short pause to breathe, soften your tone, and choose gentleness. When stress begins to rise, turn toward each other instead of pulling away. Move closer with a simple gesture such as sitting beside one another, a hand on the shoulder, or warm eye contact. Let connection gently dissolve impatience and restore calm.

20. Building Emotional Safety

"The name of the LORD is a strong tower:
the righteous runneth into it, and is safe."
Proverbs 18:10

It happened on a Thursday night, one of those quiet evenings where nothing seemed unusual on the surface. The dishes were stacked neatly beside the sink, Emeline was upstairs finishing a project, and Paldy lay on the living room rug sketching something he refused to show anyone yet. The home felt peaceful—but she didn't.

All day she had been carrying a heaviness she couldn't quite explain. It was a mixture of discouragement from something a coworker said, a moment of self-doubt she tried to brush aside, and a lingering sense of exhaustion she couldn't shake. By evening, the weight settled into her shoulders so firmly that even folding laundry felt overwhelming.

Her husband noticed before she said a word. She was quieter than usual, slower in her movements, distracted even as she stood beside him. After the kids went to bed, he found her sitting on the edge of their room, holding a pillow she'd forgotten to put into its case.

Gently he asked, "Talk to me… what's weighing on you?"

She hesitated, then saw something in his expression—steady, warm, unhurried—that made her feel safe enough to breathe. And with that safety, her heart opened. She told him everything.

And he simply held her while she spoke.

***

Emotional safety is the feeling of being able to share your inner world without fear of dismissal, judgment, or impatience. It is the comfort of knowing your heart is received gently, even when your emotions feel tangled or unclear. In marriage, emotional safety becomes the soil where trust grows and where deeper intimacy is nourished.

Creating that kind of safety begins with listening—not for the sake of responding, but for understanding. It means choosing presence instead of solutions, offering empathy rather than correction. Emotional safety is cultivated in the tone spouses use, the patience they show, and the humility with which they receive each other's emotions.

Halfway through this picture, Proverbs 18:10 provides beautiful insight. It describes God as "a strong tower" where people run to find safety. When a marriage reflects even a hint of that safe refuge, vulnerability becomes easier. Hearts begin to relax. Conversations deepen. Walls soften.

Emotional safety doesn't remove conflict, but it transforms the way conflicts are navigated. When spouses know their feelings are safe, healing becomes possible, and love grows stronger through honesty rather than silence.

***

Building emotional safety in a marriage is one of the most important investments a couple can make. It provides the foundation for trust, vulnerability, deep communication, and long-term intimacy. When emotional safety is strong, both spouses feel free to express their fears, dreams, insecurities, and hopes without worrying how the other will respond.

Emotional safety begins with consistent gentleness. Tone matters deeply. The same words delivered harshly can create distance, but spoken softly, they build closeness. A spouse who responds with patience instead of irritation communicates, "Your heart matters to me." Over time, these gentle responses form a pattern of reliability.

Listening is another essential aspect. Listening fully—without interrupting, correcting, or minimizing—tells your spouse their emotions are valid. Many couples unknowingly create emotional danger zones by rushing to fix problems rather than sitting with feelings. Safety grows when one partner says, "I hear you. Tell me more," instead of offering quick solutions.

Trust also plays a large role in emotional safety. When apologies come quickly, when forgiveness is offered sincerely, and when past vulnerabilities are never used as weapons, trust deepens. Spouses learn that honesty will be met with compassion, not punishment.

Another key is humility. Recognizing our own emotional blind spots allows us to approach our spouse with more understanding. Some people express emotions outwardly; others hold them quietly. Honoring these differences fosters acceptance rather than frustration.

Emotional safety also requires consistency. One gentle moment cannot erase weeks of sharp responses. But repeated kindness slowly rewires relational patterns. Even small actions—pausing before speaking, offering a reassuring touch, choosing slower words—can reshape the emotional climate of a home.

When emotional safety becomes a shared priority, marriage transforms. Conversations become deeper. Conflicts become more manageable. Vulnerability becomes less frightening. The home becomes a refuge where both spouses feel supported, understood, and valued.

Emotional safety is not about perfection—it's about creating a marriage where both hearts can rest unguarded and fully known.

FROM HIS PERSPECTIVE

A friend once told me something that stuck with me. He said, "My wife doesn't need me to solve her emotions—she needs me to make them safe." I didn't fully understand it at first, but over time I began to see how true it was.

When my wife trusts that I will not rush her, correct her, or tell her she's "overreacting," she opens up more freely. When I respond gently—especially when she feels fragile—it deepens our connection in ways I didn't expect.

Emotional safety from me looks like slowing down, listening without defensiveness, and speaking with warmth. It's one of the most loving things I can offer her, and it brings us closer every time I practice it.

FROM HER PERSPECTIVE

I've learned that emotional safety is not only something I receive—it's something I give. When I respond with understanding, when I choose calm instead of criticism, when I welcome my husband's thoughts without judgment, I can feel his heart relax.

Emotional safety means he doesn't have to perform strength. He can be honest. He can be human. He can be vulnerable without fear of being dismissed. Creating that space in our marriage has made our connection deeper and more tender than I expected.

PRAYER

Lord, help us create a marriage where emotional safety thrives. Teach us to listen with compassion, speak with gentleness, and protect each other's hearts with humility. Make our home a refuge of peace, comfort, and trust. Amen.

CONVERSATION PROMPTS

1. What behaviors, tones, or actions from me make you feel emotionally safe? What helps your heart open instead of shutting down?

2. Are there specific reactions of mine that have made vulnerability harder for you? How can we rebuild those moments with new patterns of understanding and gentleness?

CONNECTION PRACTICES

Share one unspoken feeling from your week, something you carried quietly. The other responds with empathy alone, offering presence instead of solutions. After sharing, use a simple physical gesture such as a hand squeeze, a hug, or brushing shoulders to communicate, "You are safe with me." Let this gentle touch reset the moment and remind you both that emotional honesty is welcome and protected in your marriage.

21. Honoring Each Other's Differences

"Be kindly affectioned one to another with
brotherly love; in honour preferring one another."
Romans 12:10

One of the most compelling real stories of honoring differences comes from the marriage of Charles and Susanna Spurgeon. Though Charles was one of the most influential preachers of the nineteenth century, his personality, pace of life, and emotional rhythms were vastly different from Susanna's. He was fiery, public, expressive, and constantly surrounded by people. Susanna, by contrast, was quieter, gentle-spirited, intellectually strong but physically fragile, and far more private.

Shortly after their marriage, Charles entered a demanding season of preaching that kept him away for long stretches. Susanna once admitted that she felt overwhelmed by his constant movement and public calling. Their personalities seemed almost opposite—his intensity beside her calm, his extroversion beside her contemplative nature.

But instead of competing, they learned to honor their differences. Charles praised Susanna's steady mind and deep compassion, calling her his "best earthly blessing." Susanna, in turn, supported his calling even when it stretched her comfort. She later said their differences strengthened them because "we leaned on each other's strengths as much as we bore each other's weaknesses."

Their marriage became a living picture of unity not built on sameness, but on honoring the unique qualities God had shaped within each of them.

***

Differences between spouses are not accidents or inconveniences. They are intentional design. God often pairs two people who see the world differently so they can strengthen one another. One may think quickly, the other more slowly. One may speak boldly, the other more gently. One may be energized by activity, the other by stillness. Differences, rather than dividing, can create balance.

But honoring differences requires humility. It means choosing curiosity instead of criticism and seeing your spouse's wiring as a gift rather than a flaw. It requires letting go of the assumption that your way is the "natural" way, and embracing the truth that God shapes each person uniquely for a reason.

Halfway into this truth, Romans 12:10 reminds us to "honor one another above yourselves." Honor is not agreement; it is respect. It means valuing the way your spouse thinks, feels, processes, and contributes—even when those patterns differ from your own.

When couples learn to honor differences, conflicts soften, appreciation grows, and unity deepens. Marriage becomes less about changing each other and more about celebrating the ways you complete each other.

***

Honoring each other's differences is one of the most powerful practices in a healthy marriage. Every couple enters marriage believing their perspective is the "normal" one. Over time, however, most spouses discover they interpret life through completely different lenses. These differences can either become lifelong sources of tension or deeply enriching strengths.

Honoring differences begins with recognizing that God created your spouse with intentionality. Their personality, pace, sensitivity, communication style, stress responses, and strengths are not accidental. They are part of God's craftsmanship. Ephesians 2:10 describes each believer as God's "workmanship." When spouses embrace that truth, they learn to view differences with reverence rather than irritation.

Differences broaden a marriage. The quieter spouse often brings reflection, stability, and emotional depth. The more assertive spouse brings courage, momentum, and problem-solving. One may be detail-oriented, while the other sees the bigger picture. One may excel in planning, while the other excels in spontaneity. These differences, when honored, create a richer, more balanced life together.

But honoring differences also requires practical effort. It means listening fully to understand—not to correct. It means learning your spouse's rhythms: what energizes them, what calms them, what overwhelms them. It means adapting rather than demanding. It means resisting the temptation to compare your spouse's strengths to someone else's or your own.

Couples who honor differences create emotional safety. They send a message that says, "You do not have to be like me to be loved well." This kind of acceptance softens defensiveness and encourages authenticity. It turns conflict into dialogue and differences into opportunities for deeper connection.

Honoring differences does not erase the challenges that come with them. Instead, it transforms the challenges into points of growth. When one spouse's weakness appears, the other's strength naturally fills the gap. When one becomes overwhelmed, the other offers balance. This interdependence strengthens trust and deepens intimacy.

When a couple learns to see their differences as God-given gifts, they stop trying to fix each other and begin to cherish each other. Honor becomes the pathway to unity.

FROM HIS PERSPECTIVE

I used to think my wife and I were incompatible because we think so differently. Now I realize that's what makes us strong. Her slower, thoughtful pace often prevented him from rushing into decisions too quickly, and my boldness helped her step into opportunities she would normally avoid.

The more I think about this the more examples I can find. My wife sees details I overlook. She senses emotional shifts I miss. She brings tenderness where I bring urgency. And although our differences used to frustrate me, I'm beginning to see how God uses them to shape me.

When I honor her unique strengths, I grow as a husband. When I appreciate her perspective, I become wiser. Our differences do not divide us; they improve us. Honoring them makes our marriage richer and more steady.

FROM HER PERSPECTIVE

I used to think our differences meant we were doing something wrong. I compared our marriage to others who seemed "more alike" and wondered why we felt opposite in so many ways. But with time, God has shown me that our differences make us stronger, not weaker.

When I feel anxious, my husband's steadiness helps me breathe. When I overthink, his clarity helps me focus. When I get discouraged, his optimism lifts me up. And my sensitivity, my nurturing spirit, and my attention to detail support him in ways he has told me matter deeply.

Honoring our differences has brought so much peace. It has helped me value who he is instead of wishing for sameness. Our marriage thrives when we lean into the beautiful variety God designed between us.

PRAYER

Lord, teach us to honor each other's differences with humility and gratitude. Help us see each other through Your eyes—crafted with purpose, designed with intention, and gifted uniquely. Strengthen our unity as we celebrate the ways we complement and refine each other. Amen.

CONVERSATION PROMPTS

1. What differences between us have been the hardest to understand, and what would help you feel more appreciated in those areas? How can we learn to see those differences as strengths rather than frustrations?

2. Which of my qualities—especially the ones different from yours—have strengthened our marriage? How can we celebrate and encourage each other's unique contributions more intentionally?

CONNECTION PRACTICES

Each of you name three differences in your spouse that you are truly grateful for, speaking them slowly and thoughtfully. Let these words honor the unique ways God has shaped each of you. Then, at some point today, notice one area where your spouse's strength differs from yours. Pause and thank them warmly for how that strength blesses your life. These simple affirmations turn differences into gifts and deepen appreciation in your marriage.

22. Rekindling Fun in Marriage

"A merry heart doeth good like a medicine:
but a broken spirit drieth the bones."
Proverbs 17:22

It started with a broom, a dustpan, and a ridiculous challenge that neither of them saw coming. The house was in Saturday-cleaning mode—laundry humming, windows open, sunlight spilling across the floors. Paldy was outside practicing soccer drills, and Emeline had disappeared into her room with music loud enough to shake the hallway.

In the middle of sweeping the kitchen, she flicked a small pile of crumbs toward him with the broom and said, "Bet you can't sweep that into the pan on the first try."

He raised an eyebrow. "Oh really?"

What happened next looked nothing like responsible adulthood. He lined up like it was an Olympic event, dramatically stretched his wrists, and—after far too much ceremony—missed horribly. She burst into laughter, and he pretended to collapse in defeat.

That single moment cracked open something they hadn't realized they were missing. The laughter lingered. The tension of the week dissolved. Before they knew it, they were working their way through the house turning ordinary chores into tiny competitions, awarding imaginary medals, laughing like they used to when they were dating.

Later that night, as they folded laundry side by side, she leaned into him and whispered, "I needed that."

Playfulness didn't fix everything—but it awakened something that had quietly fallen asleep.

***

Playfulness is often one of the first things marriages lose—not because love fades, but because responsibility grows. The weight of schedules, chores, parenting, finances, and stress slowly crowds out the simple joy of having fun together. Yet laughter, surprise, and shared delight are vital to emotional closeness.

Play brings relief to tired hearts and softness to tense atmospheres. It reminds couples that joy is not childish—it is restorative. Playfulness rekindles connection in ways words sometimes cannot. It breaks patterns of strictly "functional" communication and reopens the door to affection.

Halfway through this truth, Proverbs 17:22 shines light on the value of joy by saying, "A cheerful heart is good medicine." Laughter, inside jokes, lightheartedness—these aren't silly add-ons. They are medicine to a weary marriage. They reawaken the delight that God intended to be part of covenant love.

Playfulness doesn't ignore real problems. It simply lightens the heart so problems can be faced with more grace, patience, and unity. Couples who make room for joy find that intimacy grows naturally because their spirits remember how to rest with one another.

***

Rekindling fun and playfulness in marriage is not about pretending life is easy or ignoring serious responsibilities. It is about restoring joy to the relationship and remembering that delight is a vital part of love. Over time, many couples slip into a pattern where marriage becomes more like a partnership of tasks than a friendship of hearts. Playfulness helps reverse that drift by bringing levity, creativity, and affection back into everyday life.

Playfulness reminds couples how to enjoy one another again. It allows spouses to see their partner not just as a co-parent, provider, or planner, but as a friend. When couples laugh together, walls soften. Stress loosens. Emotional intimacy deepens because laughter invites the heart to relax. Shared joy builds memories that become anchors of connection during harder seasons.

Fun doesn't have to be elaborate. It can come from simple things: trying a new hobby together, turning mundane chores into small competitions, making spontaneous plans, revisiting an old tradition from when you were dating, or simply sharing an inside joke only the two of you understand. These small sparks revive warmth that routine can sometimes dull.

Playfulness also helps couples see each other with kindness. When spouses allow themselves to be silly, imperfect, or spontaneous, they create space for authenticity. No one has to perform. No one has to be endlessly serious. This freedom fosters a kind of vulnerability that strengthens both affection and trust.

Another important aspect of rekindling fun is intentionality. Joy rarely appears on its own in a busy household. Couples must choose it. Setting aside time, even a few minutes, to lighten the atmosphere can shift the emotional tone of the entire day. The goal is not entertainment—it is connection.

A playful marriage is not immature. It is emotionally healthy. It reflects a God who created joy, laughter, and delight. When couples intentionally nurture fun, they breathe life back into their relationship and rediscover the tender, lively connection that drew them together in the first place.

FROM HIS PERSPECTIVE

A good friend once told me that the turning point in his marriage came during a season when everything felt heavy—work stress, financial pressure, parenting challenges. One night, in the middle of dishes and chaos, he made a goofy face at his wife across the kitchen. She laughed so unexpectedly that it startled both of them.

He said, "That one laugh felt like oxygen."

After that, he began doing small things—playful teasing, silly notes, spontaneous small adventures. His wife responded in ways he hadn't seen in years. Joy slowly returned, not because they solved everything, but because they remembered how to enjoy each other again.

That story taught me something important: sometimes the most spiritual thing I can do is help us laugh. Playfulness is not immaturity—it is presence. It is choosing delight instead of distance.

FROM HER PERSPECTIVE

I'm realizing that playfulness is one of the simplest ways to keep our marriage warm. When we laugh together, I feel closer to him. When we do something silly or spontaneous, part of me wakes up again. Fun doesn't replace responsibility—it refreshes me so I can handle responsibility with more grace.

I want our marriage to feel light enough for joy and safe enough for silliness. Playfulness reminds me that our relationship is a gift to enjoy, not only a job to manage.

PRAYER

Lord, help us rediscover joy in our marriage. Teach us to laugh together, to play together, and to cherish the lighthearted moments You give us. Restore any places where joy has faded and fill our home with a spirit of warmth, connection, and delight. Amen.

CONVERSATION PROMPTS

1. What kinds of fun made you feel closest to me earlier in our marriage, and which of those activities or rhythms would you love to revive now?

2. What prevents us from being playful—stress, exhaustion, busyness, or feeling disconnected? How can we gently remove those barriers so joy becomes part of our daily life again?

CONNECTION PRACTICES

Set a timer for five minutes and share a simple moment of joy together. Watch a funny video, try a tiny challenge, play a quick game, or do anything lighthearted that brings laughter into the room. Keep it easy and playful, focusing more on connection than performance. Let the shared laughter loosen any tension from the day and remind you both that delight, even in small doses, strengthens the bond you are building together.

23. Relearning Tenderness

"Put on therefore, as the elect of God,
holy and beloved, bowels of mercies, kindness,
humbleness of mind, meekness, longsuffering."
Colossians 3:12

It happened after one of those exhausting weeks—the kind that spills over into irritation before either spouse realizes it. Work had been stressful for both of us. The kids had been pushing boundaries. The house felt chaotic, and every conversation seemed to brush against some raw edge neither of us had the energy to soften.

On Friday night, my wife dropped her bag at the door and sighed without meaning to. I was standing at the counter sorting mail, trying to finish a task I'd started three times already.

Later that evening, when the house finally quieted, they sat on opposite ends of the couch—close, but not really connected. She stared at her hands. I stared at the floor. Finally, she whispered, "I miss us."

I looked up. I scooted across the couch, wrapped his arm around her, and said, "I'm sorry we let the week get to us." Something warm returned in that moment.

***

Tenderness is often one of the first qualities a marriage quietly loses—not from malice, but from fatigue. Responsibilities pile up. Stress tightens emotions. Words become more functional and less gentle. Tenderness fades slowly, almost unnoticed, until one day a couple feels distant without knowing why.

Relearning tenderness means returning to small, gentle acts that communicate, "Your heart matters to me." It is the tone of voice chosen during a difficult conversation, the softening of posture when tensions rise, the kindness offered even when emotions run high. Tenderness is not weakness; it is controlled strength expressed with love.

Halfway through this truth, Colossians 3:12 gives powerful direction: "Clothe yourselves with compassion, kindness, humility, gentleness, and patience." These qualities are a posture of the heart—a choice to move toward your spouse with grace, especially when the week feels heavy.

Tenderness does not erase conflict, but it transforms the atmosphere in which conflict takes place. When couples relearn tenderness, emotional walls come down, misunderstandings shrink, and trust grows. Tenderness restores warmth that distance tries to steal.

***

Relearning tenderness is an essential discipline in marriage. Tenderness is the gentle touch of love expressed through tone, posture, presence, and sensitivity. When couples first fall in love, tenderness flows effortlessly. A soft word, a warm glance, a reassuring touch—these gestures are instinctive. But as life grows heavier, tenderness can slowly fade beneath layers of routine, responsibility, and stress.

Tenderness must be intentionally cultivated. It requires awareness, noticing when your spouse seems overwhelmed or discouraged. It demands softness in moments where frustration might feel easier. It calls for patience instead of defensiveness, especially when emotions are strained. Tenderness is the decision to treat your spouse's heart as fragile, valuable, and worthy of gentleness—even in difficult seasons.

One of the reasons tenderness matters so deeply is because it shapes emotional safety. A marriage saturated with tenderness creates a place where vulnerability feels welcomed. A spouse will share more openly when they feel heard, soothed, and valued rather than rushed or criticized. Tenderness is a soothing balm that calms tension and reminds each partner that they are loved not just in grand gestures, but in the delicate daily moments that knit a relationship together.

Tenderness also prevents emotional drift. Harsh tones, hurried conversations, and unfiltered reactions build quiet walls over time. But small acts of gentleness steadily dismantle those walls. A gentle touch on the back, a soft "I'm sorry," an affectionate glance across the room—these simple gestures bring warmth back into the relationship.

Practicing tenderness also deepens empathy. It helps each spouse pause long enough to ask, "What might they be feeling right now?" This question shifts the marriage toward understanding rather than assumption. It encourages compassion instead of criticism.

Finally, tenderness reflects the heart of God. Scripture repeatedly describes Him as compassionate, slow to anger, and rich in love. When spouses practice tenderness, they mirror His gentleness to one another, building a home where His peace can flourish.

Relearning tenderness is not about perfection—it is about practicing softness that strengthens love daily.

FROM HIS PERSPECTIVE

A friend of mine shared a moment that stayed with me. He said his wife came home from work looking completely worn out. He was tired too, and his first instinct was to retreat into silence. Instead, something nudged him to walk over, place his hand lightly on her back, and whisper, "Rough day?" She melted into his arms and cried—a release she didn't even know she needed.

He told me, "It took me five seconds of tenderness to shift her whole evening."

Hearing that made me realize how often I underestimate the impact of small gentle moments. Tenderness doesn't require energy or planning—it only requires noticing. When I approach my wife with softness, it draws us together almost instantly. Tenderness is one of the most powerful tools I have to communicate love.

FROM HER PERSPECTIVE

I'm learning that tenderness is often a choice, not a feeling. When I slow down, soften my voice, and reach for my husband with gentleness, our connection strengthens instantly. Tenderness helps me express love without forcing big moments. Sometimes it's as simple as meeting his eyes or touching his hand. Tenderness brings warmth back into our relationship and makes everyday moments feel meaningful again.

PRAYER

Lord, help us relearn tenderness. Teach us to soften our voices, our reactions, and our hearts toward one another. Fill our marriage with gentleness that restores connection and reflects Your kindness. Amen.

CONVERSATION PROMPTS

1. What actions, tones, or gestures feel tender to you? Which ones make you feel seen, cared for, and emotionally comforted?

2. What situations make tenderness harder for you to give or receive? How can we support each other during those moments so gentleness becomes natural again?

CONNECTION PRACTICES

Take five minutes to share something lighthearted together, whether a funny video, a tiny game, or a playful challenge. Let simple joy soften the day. Then practice beginning every conversation with gentleness, using a warm tone, a kind posture, or a brief affirmation before speaking. Soft beginnings create safe endings. Together, these two small choices help reset the emotional atmosphere of your home and deepen your sense of closeness and ease with one another.

24. Protecting Your Home from Busyness

"Be still, and know that I am God: I will be exalted among the heathen, I will be exalted in the earth."
Psalm 46:10

One of the most revealing true stories about Jonathan Edwards involves the demanding years of his ministry and the extraordinary tenderness of his wife, Sarah Edwards. Edwards was a brilliant preacher, writer, and theologian, but his schedule was often overwhelming—sermons, visitors, correspondence, meetings, and responsibilities that stretched him thin.

There was a season recorded in their family's writings when the busyness of ministry nearly consumed him. His mind raced constantly, his duties multiplied, and his exhaustion became visible even to the children. The home felt the weight of his pace.

Sarah recognized the signs. Rather than scolding or resenting the demands placed on her husband, she quietly created pockets of rest around him. She began preparing simple moments of stillness—a warm meal left waiting, a short walk outdoors, a candlelit room where he could think and pray undisturbed. Her gentleness softened the frantic edge that busyness had created.

One evening, Edwards returned home utterly drained. Sarah welcomed him with quiet warmth, saying only, "You may rest here." He later wrote that her calming presence "restored to me the sweetness of home."

Their story reminds us that busyness, if left unchecked, slowly suffocates tenderness, clarity, and connection. Protecting the home from busyness is an act of love.

***

Busyness often enters a home disguised as responsibility. Tasks pile up, schedules tighten, and the pace of life slowly pushes out peace. When a home becomes dominated by hurry, emotional connection thins, conversations shorten, and tenderness fades. Spouses begin functioning like coworkers rather than companions.

Protecting the home from busyness requires conscious slowing. It means choosing presence over productivity when your spouse needs your attention, pausing long enough to listen, and creating small rhythms of rest. Slowness becomes a gift you give to each other.

Halfway through this truth, Psalm 46:10 speaks with clear simplicity: "Be still, and know that I am God." Stillness is not inactivity. It is a posture of trust that reorders priorities. When a couple chooses stillness—shared quiet, slower meals, gentler conversations—they make room for God's peace to settle into their home.

Busyness will always compete for space. But couples who guard their home's pace find that connection deepens, patience grows, and emotional safety strengthens. Protecting the home from busyness is one of the most powerful ways to protect the marriage itself.

***

Busyness is more than a full calendar—it is a speed of life that crowds out connection.

A marriage cannot thrive when both spouses are constantly rushing, reacting, or surviving the day. Protecting the home from busyness begins with recognizing that emotional presence matters more than constant activity. A quiet five minutes of genuine connection can strengthen a marriage more than an entire day spent moving side by side without noticing one another.

One of the dangers of busyness is that it numbs awareness. Spouses stop noticing small signals—fatigue in the eyes, tension in the shoulders, sadness hiding behind forced smiles. When hearts are hurried, empathy fades. Conversations become shallow. Tenderness becomes rare. Busyness convinces couples that slowing down is a luxury, when in reality it is a necessity for emotional health.

Protecting the home from busyness means intentionally reducing the noise. It may look like choosing fewer commitments, creating device-free moments, or establishing small rituals of pause: a slow morning prayer together, a peaceful meal, a shared evening walk. These practices re-center the marriage and create space for deeper connection.

Another key to resisting busyness is learning to rest without guilt. Many spouses feel pressure to stay productive, but marriage thrives when rest becomes part of the rhythm. Rest invites vulnerability, softness, and conversation. It creates an atmosphere where emotional honesty can flourish.

Slowing the pace also means setting boundaries. Couples must learn to say no—to unnecessary obligations, draining relationships, and activities that erode peace. Protecting the home is an act of stewardship, guarding the emotional climate so love can grow.

Finally, protecting the home from busyness invites God back into the center. A hurried life easily forgets His presence, but a slower home becomes fertile ground for prayer, gratitude, and spiritual clarity. Peace settles where hurry once ruled.

A marriage that resists busyness becomes a sanctuary—a place where burdens lift, hearts breathe, and love grows deeper through every season.

***

FROM HIS PERSPECTIVE

A close friend once told me he didn't realize how hurried his life had become until his wife said gently, "I miss your eyes." She didn't mean they were gone—she meant he no longer slowed down long enough to really look at her. He was always preparing for the next thing, racing through conversations, and moving quickly from task to task.

That sentence changed him. He began to notice how much his busyness shaped the emotional tone of their home. When he rushed, everyone felt rushed. When he slowed down, warmth returned. He told me, "My pace was hurting my marriage more than any conflict."

Hearing his experience made me look at our own home. I realized how easily I get caught up in tasks, plans, and responsibilities. When I hurry, my tone sharpens. My patience thins. My wife becomes someone I "get back to" instead of someone I notice in the moment. But when I slow down—even briefly—I feel the whole atmosphere shift. Protecting our home from busyness has become one of my most important roles. My pace affects more than my schedule; it affects her heart.

FROM HER PERSPECTIVE

Busyness sneaks into my heart before I notice it. I start thinking about everything that needs to be done, and soon my mind races faster than my body. When I become hurried, I'm more easily frustrated, more distracted, and less emotionally present with my husband. I don't intend to push him aside—life just becomes loud.

But I've learned that when I choose to slow down, even slightly, connection returns. A quiet moment sitting together, a slower conversation, or a few minutes of shared rest softens my whole spirit. Busyness makes me feel alone; slowing down makes me feel close again.

I want our home to be a peaceful place, not a rushed one. Protecting it from busyness requires intention—but the intimacy it brings is worth every effort.

PRAYER

Lord, teach us to guard our home from the grip of busyness. Help us slow our pace, notice each other's hearts, and make room for peace. Give us wisdom to set healthy boundaries, courage to say no when needed, and grace to rest without guilt. Fill our home with stillness that brings clarity, tenderness, and renewed connection. Let our marriage reflect the calm of Your presence and the quiet strength of Your love. Amen.

CONVERSATION PROMPTS

1. When does busyness affect you the most—emotionally, physically, or spiritually? How do you feel it impacts the way we talk, connect, or rest together? What specific signs should I look for that tell me you're becoming overwhelmed, and how can I respond in a way that helps you feel supported instead of pressured?

2. Which parts of our routine make our home feel rushed or stressed? Are there commitments, habits, or patterns that steal our peace? What practical changes—big or small—could we make to slow the atmosphere of our home so connection becomes easier and more natural?

CONNECTION PRACTICES

Choose one moment today to intentionally slow down together—sit quietly, hold hands, breathe deeply, or enjoy five minutes without devices. Then identify one small source of busyness you can remove or adjust this week. Celebrate the peaceful space you create.

25. Deepening Your Prayer Life as a Couple

"Again I say to you that if two of you agree
on earth concerning anything that they ask,
it will be done for them by My Father in heaven."
Matthew 18:19

On one morning, you'd find on the dusty road to Emmaus two disciples walking with heavy hearts after the crucifixion of Christ. They had heard rumors of resurrection, but disappointment clouded their understanding. As they walked, they talked quietly, processing grief, confusion, and hope all at once. Into that private conversation, the risen Jesus appeared without them recognizing Him.

But Jesus didn't preach immediately. He didn't overwhelm them with miracles. Instead, He walked with them, listened to them, and gently drew their hearts back toward faith. Their confusion became conversation. Their sorrow became prayer. Their questions became communion.

When they finally reached their lodging and invited Him to stay, Jesus broke bread, and their eyes were opened. They recognized Him in a moment of shared fellowship—an encounter that transformed their despair into joy. They later said, "Did not our hearts burn within us as He talked with us on the road?"

Their story reveals something profound: when two believers walk together, speak honestly, and invite Jesus into their shared space, their hearts are strengthened. Prayer doesn't always begin with kneeling. It often begins with walking, talking, and welcoming Christ into the ordinary moments.

***

Praying as a couple can feel intimidating at first. Many spouses worry about saying the wrong words, praying imperfectly, or feeling vulnerable. But shared prayer is not about eloquence—it is about unity. It is the simple act of placing your hearts before God together, trusting that He listens to both the spoken and the unspoken.

Prayer strengthens a marriage by aligning two hearts with God's heart. It softens tension, redirects focus, and brings clarity where confusion once lived. Praying together builds intimacy because it opens the deepest parts of the soul—hopes, fears, desires, and weaknesses.

Halfway into this truth, Matthew 18:19 gives a powerful promise: "If two of you agree on earth about anything they ask, it will be done for them." God honors agreement. He blesses unity. He draws near when couples seek Him together.

Prayer doesn't remove challenges, but it changes how couples face them. When spouses bring their concerns to God, fear loses its grip and peace takes its place. A shared prayer life becomes the spiritual anchor that holds the marriage steady through every season.

***

Deepening your prayer life as a couple builds a spiritual foundation that strengthens every part of your marriage. Prayer isn't meant to be complicated or formal; it is a conversation with God that grows richer over time. When couples choose to pray together consistently, they create a sacred place where their hearts can be honest, their relationship can be refined, and their unity can deepen.

One of the greatest barriers to shared prayer is vulnerability. Praying aloud exposes inner fears, desires, and struggles. It invites your spouse into the places you usually guard. But that vulnerability becomes the soil where intimacy grows. When you pray together, you allow your spouse to witness your faith, your hopes, and even your weaknesses. This transparency creates a profound spiritual closeness.

Another barrier is intimidation. Many spouses feel unqualified or awkward praying aloud. But God is not listening for polished speech; He is listening for sincerity. A simple, quiet prayer said with humility draws heaven closer than the most poetic phrases spoken without heart.

Deepening your prayer life begins with small rhythms—praying before meals, praying before bed, praying during stress or conflict, or offering brief prayers throughout the day. These small choices slowly build a habit of spiritual unity. Over time, prayer becomes as natural as breathing, a refuge you both run to rather than a duty you perform.

Shared prayer also strengthens decision-making. Couples who seek God together find clarity faster because they are listening to the same Shepherd. When God's peace rests on a decision, unity follows.

Finally, praying together invites God's presence into your home. It transforms the emotional atmosphere, reduces tension, and awakens gratitude. Prayer softens hearts and aligns priorities. It reminds couples that their marriage is built not on their own strength, but on God's sustaining grace.

A marriage rooted in prayer becomes a partnership of faith—strong, steady, and deeply connected.

***

FROM HIS PERSPECTIVE

I used to feel nervous praying aloud with my wife. I worried my words wouldn't sound "spiritual enough." But one evening, after a difficult week, she simply took my hand and whispered, "Pray with me." I didn't have a script. I didn't feel profound. Yet as I stumbled through a simple prayer, something in me softened. She squeezed my hand gently, and I realized prayer wasn't performance—it was presence.

A friend once told me that praying with his wife changed the way he saw her. He said, "When she prays, I see her heart in a way I never could before." That sentence stuck with me. Prayer reveals the tender spaces we sometimes hide. It also builds unity in a way nothing else can.

Now, when I pray with my wife, even for a minute, I feel more grounded. My anxieties loosen. My priorities reorder. And I feel closer to her. Prayer doesn't have to be long or eloquent. It just has to be shared. Each time we pray, even briefly, our marriage feels steadier—rooted in something greater than both of us.

FROM HER PERSPECTIVE

Praying with my husband has become one of the most intimate parts of our relationship—not because the prayers are perfect, but because they are honest. When he prays for us, I feel protected. When he whispers a simple prayer during a stressful moment, I feel steadier. Prayer brings a softness to our connection that words alone cannot create.

I've learned that prayer invites me to slow down, breathe, and remember that God cares about every detail of our marriage. It draws us back to unity when we drift apart. It makes me feel seen and loved in ways that surprise me. Shared prayer has become a refuge—a sacred rhythm that helps us navigate life with greater peace and tenderness.

PRAYER

Lord, teach us to seek You together with humility and trust. Help us overcome any fear, hesitation, or insecurity about praying as one. Draw our hearts into unity as we lift our concerns, dreams, and needs before You. Strengthen our connection through every shared prayer, and let Your peace rest on our home. Guide our steps, soften our hearts, and tune our spirits to Your voice. Make prayer the steady rhythm that deepens our love and anchors our marriage in Your presence. Amen.

CONVERSATION PROMPTS

1. What makes praying together feel comfortable or uncomfortable for you? Are there fears, insecurities, or past experiences that shape how you approach prayer? How can I support you and make praying together feel safer, more natural, and more meaningful? Tell me what kinds of prayer moments feel easiest to begin.

2. What areas of our life do you most want us to bring before God—finances, parenting, decisions, fears, or our emotional connection? How can we make space for regular prayer without feeling forced or rushed? Which small prayer habits could strengthen our unity?

CONNECTION PRACTICES

Choose one moment today to pray together for one minute—no pressure, no format, just sincerity. Then pick a small daily rhythm to maintain for the week: a short bedtime prayer, a quick morning blessing, or a prayer before facing a stressful task. Let these simple moments deepen your unity.

26. Being Quick to Listen

"Wherefore, my beloved brethren, let every man
be swift to hear, slow to speak, slow to wrath."
James 1:19

It happened on an ordinary school morning, the kind where everything feels slightly rushed. Emeline was searching for a missing project, Paldy was moving at half-speed, and breakfast was cooling on the table. Tension hovered in the air like a low cloud. She was packing lunches while mentally organizing her workday. He was trying to fix a loose shoelace while answering an early text from a coworker.

Then it started—small frustrations spoken a little too quickly.

"Didn't we talk about being ready on time?"

"Why are we always rushed?"

"Can someone please just help me find my folder?"

No one was yelling, but the tone felt sharp enough to bruise. In the middle of the chaos, he stepped into the hallway and found Emeline near tears, clutching her backpack straps. When he asked what was wrong, she whispered, "I feel like no one hears me."

Her words hit him harder than the rush of the morning.

After school drop-off, he came home and found his wife at the kitchen table. Instead of explaining, defending, or solving, he sat down beside her and said softly, "Tell me what you were feeling this morning. I'm listening."

That sentence changed everything.

The noise quieted.

The distance shrank.

Listening restored peace.

***

Listening is one of the simplest acts of love, yet one of the hardest to practice consistently. In marriage, moments of stress, fatigue, or misunderstanding can tempt spouses to react quickly rather than listen carefully. But listening—true, patient, compassionate listening—creates space for vulnerability, honesty, and emotional connection.

When a spouse feels heard, their defenses soften. Confusion becomes clarity. Frustration becomes understanding. But when listening disappears, assumptions grow, and distance quietly forms.

Halfway into this truth, James 1:19 offers essential wisdom: "Everyone should be quick to listen, slow to speak, and slow to become angry." This verse is not about silence; it is about attention. It invites spouses to approach each conversation with humility rather than hurry.

Being quick to listen means pausing before responding. It means setting aside distractions, leaning in, and giving weight to your spouse's emotional world. Listening says, "Your voice matters to me."

When couples learn this skill, conflicts de-escalate faster, tenderness grows, and the marriage becomes a safe place for the heart to speak freely.

***

Being quick to listen strengthens the emotional foundation of a marriage. Listening is more than hearing words—it is receiving the heart behind them. It requires attention, patience, humility, and a genuine desire to understand. When spouses practice listening intentionally, they communicate value, respect, and compassion.

Listening slows the pace of conflict. When arguments arise, the temptation to defend or correct is strong. But when one spouse pauses and listens without interruption, the emotional tone shifts. The conversation becomes less about winning and more about connecting. Many misunderstandings disappear simply because one spouse felt heard.

Listening also builds trust. When someone knows their thoughts and emotions will not be dismissed, minimized, or rushed, they open up more freely. This openness deepens intimacy and strengthens the bond of the marriage. Over time, listening becomes a form of emotional protection—a way of saying, "I am safe for your heart."

Being quick to listen requires eliminating distractions. Phones, tasks, screens, and mental overload make it difficult to give full attention. Couples strengthen listening by intentionally creating uncluttered moments: turning toward each other during conversations, making eye contact, pausing household tasks, or setting aside time to talk without interruption.

Humility is also essential. Listening means accepting that your spouse's perspective is valid even when you see things differently. Instead of planning your response, you lean into their experience. Instead of assuming motives, you seek clarification. This humility softens conflict and builds mutual respect.

Finally, listening mirrors the heart of Christ. Scripture describes Him as compassionate, gentle, and attentive to those who cried out to Him. When spouses listen with patience and tenderness, they reflect His love.

Being quick to listen transforms the emotional climate of the marriage. It turns conversations into pathways of understanding and strengthens unity in every season.

***

FROM HIS PERSPECTIVE

I used to jump too quickly into explanations. If my wife shared something difficult, I'd immediately try to fix it, clarify it, or defend myself. I thought I was helping. But one day she said softly, "I need you to hear me before you answer me." Those words stopped me. I realized I was filling the space with solutions when what she needed was presence.

A friend once told me something similar. He said his marriage changed the day he realized listening was more powerful than speaking. During an argument, instead of pushing back, he simply said, "I want to understand you—help me hear your heart." His wife broke down in tears because she felt seen instead of challenged.

Listening takes humility. It means putting aside my instinct to fix or defend. When I really listen—without forming my response in advance—I feel our hearts move closer. She relaxes. I soften. The whole atmosphere shifts. Now, when we talk, I remind myself: she isn't asking me to solve everything. She's asking me to care.

FROM HER PERSPECTIVE

Listening has taught me to slow my reactions. Sometimes I jump to conclusions or assume his meaning before he finishes speaking. I've learned that when I pause and truly listen, I hear not just his words but his heart. And most of the time, his heart is softer than I assumed.

When he listens to me without interrupting, something inside me settles. I feel valued. I feel understood. I feel safe. Listening turns conflict into connection. It removes defensiveness and builds trust. And when I offer him the same patience, our conversations become gentle instead of sharp. Listening is a gift we give each other—one that brings peace back into our home.

PRAYER

Lord, teach us to be quick to listen and slow to speak. Help us quiet our reactions, soften our tones, and make space for each other's hearts. Give us patience to understand before responding and humility to value one another's perspectives. Fill our home with gentleness so our conversations lead to unity rather than distance. Shape our marriage into a place where both of us feel heard, known, and deeply loved. Amen.

CONVERSATION PROMPTS

1. When do you feel most listened to by me—during quiet moments, during conflict, or when you're sharing something emotional? What helps you feel fully heard, and what makes listening difficult for you? Help me understand how I can be more present during our conversations.

2. What are the biggest obstacles that keep us from listening well—busyness, stress, assumptions, or distractions? How can we gently remove those barriers? What practical changes would make our conversations calmer and more connected?

CONNECTION PRACTICES

Choose one conversation today to practice intentional listening. Sit facing each other, maintain eye contact, and let one spouse speak uninterrupted for two minutes. Then switch. Close the moment by expressing one thing you heard that mattered.

27. Choosing Humility Over Pride

"Let nothing be done through strife or vainglory; but in lowliness of mind let each esteem other better than themselves."
Philippians 2:3

During the final hours of Jesus' earthly ministry, the disciples had gathered for the Passover meal. The room held a mixture of anticipation, confusion, and unspoken tension. They took their places around the table, each one aware of the sacredness of the moment yet unaware of the lesson Jesus was about to teach.

During the meal, Jesus rose from the table, wrapped a towel around His waist, poured water into a basin, and began washing the feet of each disciple. This act startled them. Foot washing was the work of a servant. It was the lowest task in a household, often done by someone with little social standing. Yet here was the Messiah, the One they believed to be the Son of God, kneeling before fishermen and tax collectors.

Peter resisted at first, unable to imagine his Teacher stooping so low. Jesus responded gently, explaining that the humility being shown was something they would need in order to serve each other. When He finished, He said, "I have set you an example that you should do as I have done for you."

This story reveals a truth that shapes every marriage. Humility is not weakness. It is strength that chooses love over pride every time.

***

Humility is one of the most powerful attitudes in marriage. It opens the heart to understanding, reduces conflict, and strengthens emotional closeness. Pride pushes couples apart by creating defensiveness, stubbornness, or a desire to win. Humility draws them together by creating space for gentleness, honesty, and compassion.

Choosing humility means accepting that both spouses are continually growing. It also means recognizing that disagreements do not require a victory. They require love. Humility allows a spouse to listen without needing to be right, to apologize without needing justification, and to respond softly even when emotions feel strong.

Halfway into this truth, Philippians 2:3 gives clear direction. "Do nothing out of selfish ambition or vain conceit. Rather, in humility value others above yourselves." When applied to marriage, this verse encourages spouses to place each other's needs above prideful impulses.

Humility is not self neglect. It is self control. When a couple chooses humility, they create an atmosphere that is safe for vulnerability and rich in grace. It transforms the tone of conversations, helps repair misunderstandings, and strengthens the bond between husband and wife.

***

Choosing humility over pride is one of the most essential habits for a healthy marriage. Pride often appears quietly. It hides in interruptions during conversations, in the refusal to apologize, and in the desire to protect one's own perspective at the cost of connection. Over time, pride builds emotional walls that make communication harder and misunderstandings more painful. Humility gently removes those walls.

Humility begins with a willingness to listen before reacting. When a spouse listens with patience, they communicate respect. They create a space where the other feels valued, even during conflict. Listening is one of the clearest expressions of humility because it acknowledges that the other person deserves to be heard.

Another aspect of humility is the readiness to apologize. Apologies that come quickly and sincerely prevent bitterness from settling. When spouses admit fault without excuses, they build trust. They show that preserving unity matters more than preserving ego. Apologizing is not about defeat. It is about choosing connection over distance.

Humility is also seen in small sacrifices. It might mean choosing kindness during a stressful moment, slowing down to offer support, or letting go of the need to win every disagreement. These small choices add up to a significant impact on emotional intimacy.

Practicing humility requires intentional effort. It asks both spouses to recognize their own limitations and receive grace. It also invites them to extend grace to one another. Instead of keeping score or focusing on weaknesses, humility chooses compassion. It protects the heart from harshness and guards the marriage from unnecessary tension.

Finally, humility reflects the example of Christ. Scripture shows Him continually serving with gentleness. When spouses treat each other with this same posture, they bring God's peace into their home. A marriage shaped by humility is a marriage where trust grows, tenderness thrives, and love matures in every season.

***

FROM HIS PERSPECTIVE

I have realized that pride often shows up in the smallest moments. Sometimes it comes when I want to explain before listening. Other times it shows up when I want to defend my actions instead of acknowledging my wife's feelings. Pride makes me focus on myself, but humility helps me focus on us.

A friend shared a story with me that I will never forget. He said he once had a long argument with his wife, both of them exhausted and frustrated. After hours of going in circles, he suddenly felt convicted to stop trying to win. Instead of continuing, he walked over, sat beside her, and said, "I do not want this to separate us. I am sorry." He told me that her entire posture changed. The tension dissolved. Humility ended what pride was keeping alive.

His experience taught me something. Humility does not weaken a man. It frees him. When I choose humility, I feel lighter. I feel closer to my wife. I feel peace return to our home. When I let go of the need to be right, love takes the lead again.

FROM HER PERSPECTIVE

I am learning that humility in marriage means softening my heart even when I feel hurt or misunderstood. Sometimes I want to defend myself or prove a point. But when I step back and choose humility, the atmosphere shifts. My tone softens. My patience grows. My husband feels safer sharing his thoughts.

Humility helps me see him more clearly. Instead of assuming motives, I begin to notice his effort and his tenderness. When I apologize or listen carefully, he opens up more. Humility strengthens our bond because it invites both of us to show up with honesty and grace.

Humility does not erase disagreements, but it transforms them into opportunities for connection. It reminds me that we are partners, not opponents. When I choose humility, I feel God's peace in our home.

PRAYER

Lord, teach us to lay aside pride and clothe ourselves with humility. Help us listen with patience, speak with gentleness, and respond with compassion. Give us the courage to apologize quickly and the grace to forgive freely. Shape our hearts so that our marriage reflects Your kindness and peace. Strengthen us to choose connection over stubbornness and unity over self protection. Let humility guide our steps and deepen our love each day. Amen.

CONVERSATION PROMPTS

1. When does pride show up the most for you during our conversations or disagreements? What situations make it hard to choose humility, and how can I support you in those moments so that you feel safe enough to soften and speak openly without fear of rejection or misunderstanding?

2. What are specific ways we can practice humility more intentionally in our daily interactions? Are there patterns, habits, or tones that we should adjust? How can we remind each other gently when pride begins to take over so we can return to a posture of grace and connection?

CONNECTION PRACTICES

Choose one moment today to practice humility intentionally. Offer a soft apology, listen without interrupting, or affirm your spouse's feelings before sharing your own. At the end of the day, share one example where you noticed humility strengthening your connection.

28. Strengthening Your Spiritual Bond

"And Enoch walked with God after he begat Methuselah
three hundred years, and begat sons and daughters"
Genesis 5:24

The night was unnervingly still. The sky hung low and heavy, as if holding its breath. A single figure walked along the ridge with deliberate steps, his silhouette cutting through the pale starlight. No one knew where he was going. No one dared follow. But it was said that when Enoch walked at night, the very earth seemed to listen.

Villagers whispered stories about him. Some claimed he prayed until the air changed. Others said he spoke with God in ways no one could explain. Children watched from doorways as he passed, sensing something different in the way he moved. Even the elders lowered their voices when his name came up.

Enoch never performed dramatic miracles. He lived quietly, worked faithfully, and walked with God in a way so steady that his presence seemed to soften the world around him. His walk with God was not a single moment but a lifelong rhythm. Step after step. Day after day. A bond built through nearness rather than noise.

One evening, he walked into the hills as usual. He did not return. Scripture simply says, "God took him." There was no spectacle, no warning. Just a deep spiritual bond so close that God drew him into His presence forever.

***

Enoch's life demonstrates what it looks like to build a spiritual bond through steady, daily nearness to God. His walk was not dramatic or public. It was patient, consistent, and intimate. Scripture gives only a small glimpse of his life, yet that glimpse reveals something powerful. Enoch stayed close to God, and God stayed close to him.

Strengthening your spiritual bond as a couple is similar. It is built through small moments of shared faith rather than grand gestures. Praying together, reading Scripture together, and inviting God into daily decisions slowly weave spiritual unity between two hearts.

Halfway into this truth, Genesis 5:24 offers a simple yet extraordinary statement. "Enoch walked faithfully with God." Faithfulness, not perfection, is what deepens spiritual connection.

A couple who walks with God together becomes steadier, wiser, and more tender toward each other. Spiritual closeness softens pride, strengthens communication, and increases peace. When your walk with God becomes a shared journey, your marriage gains an anchor no circumstance can shake.

***

Strengthening your spiritual bond as a couple creates a foundation that influences every part of your marriage. Spiritual unity does not happen by accident. It grows through shared focus, shared faith, and shared rhythms that draw two hearts toward God and toward each other. A couple that seeks God together becomes increasingly aligned in values, purpose, and direction. Their marriage becomes anchored in something greater than personal preference or emotion.

A strong spiritual bond brings clarity during confusion. When both spouses turn to Scripture and prayer, they hear the same truth. This alignment reduces conflict and increases trust. Instead of relying solely on personal perspectives, you learn to seek God's wisdom as a team. Decisions become easier when both hearts move toward the same source of guidance.

Spiritual unity also deepens emotional intimacy. When a couple prays together, reads together, or talks honestly about what God is teaching them, they reveal vulnerable parts of their hearts. This transparency builds closeness. It helps each spouse see the inner world of the other. A strong spiritual life invites gentleness, humility, and compassion into the relationship.

Another benefit of a spiritual bond is resilience. Difficult seasons do not break couples who lean on God as one. They pray instead of panic. They support instead of withdraw. They return to Scripture instead of reacting impulsively. Spiritual habits help couples stay steady even when the world feels uncertain.

Finally, a shared spiritual life transforms the home environment. Peace becomes more natural. Grace becomes the primary language. Moments of tension resolve more quickly because both spouses want to honor God in the way they treat each other. A strong spiritual bond does not create perfection, but it creates direction. It shapes a marriage that grows deeper, softer, and stronger with time.

FROM HIS PERSPECTIVE

One of the messages at our wedding day really shared with me. Emeline's mentor said that the greatest turning point in his marriage came not from a dramatic moment but from a slow shift. He and his wife began praying together every night, even when they were tired. At first the prayers were short and awkward. He said he stumbled over words and worried he sounded foolish. But they kept going.

Over time, he found himself opening up in ways he never had before. He began to share his fears, his hopes, and the quiet places where he struggled. His wife listened with a tenderness he had never noticed fully. He told us that praying together made him feel more connected to her than any date night or vacation ever had. Their hearts grew closer each time they sought God together.

Hearing his story made me realize that spiritual connection does not require perfect prayers or long sessions. It requires presence. When I pray with my wife or read a verse with her, I feel the same quiet closeness. It anchors me. It strengthens our unity. It reminds me that we are walking through life together with God at our side.

FROM HER PERSPECTIVE

I have noticed that our spiritual bond grows strongest during the simplest moments. Sometimes it is when we pause to pray before a stressful day. Sometimes it is when he reads a verse aloud and we talk about it for a minute. Sometimes it is when we quietly thank God for something good He has done.

These small moments remind me that God is present in our marriage, guiding us, soothing us, and drawing us closer. When we seek Him together, I feel a deeper peace. My heart becomes steadier. My love for my husband becomes gentler and more grounded. Spiritual closeness makes me feel safe with him and safe with God at the same time.

PRAYER

Lord, strengthen our spiritual bond. Teach us to walk with You together in the quiet moments as well as the challenging ones. Help us pray with sincerity, listen for Your guidance, and support each other with grace. Draw our hearts closer to You so they grow closer to each other. Shape our home into a place where Your peace rests and Your presence leads us. Make our faith steady, humble, and united. Amen.

CONVERSATION PROMPTS

1. When do you feel closest to God as a couple? Are there habits or moments that help your heart open more easily? How can we create more space for those rhythms in our daily routine so our spiritual bond grows stronger and more natural?

2. What parts of our spiritual life feel difficult or unfamiliar? Is there anything that makes praying or reading together uncomfortable? How can we support each other in growing spiritually without pressure or comparison?

CONNECTION PRACTICES

Choose one simple spiritual rhythm to practice today: a shared prayer, reading a short passage, or thanking God together for three blessings. Keep it peaceful and easy. End the day by sharing one way you sensed God's presence in your marriage.

29. Embracing a Servant Heart

"For even the Son of man came not to be ministered unto,
but to minister, and to give his life a ransom for many."
Mark 10:45

The hallway of the orphan house was quiet, the kind of quiet that settles after a long day of caring for dozens of children. George Muller walked slowly through the rows of small beds, pausing to straighten a blanket here and smooth a pillow there. The lantern he carried cast a soft glow over the room, illuminating tired faces resting peacefully.

Visitors often imagined that his influence came from his preaching or his leadership. But those who lived with him saw something different. They saw a man who served quietly when no one watched. They saw him wash cups, mend clothing, carry sick children, and pray over each bed with a tenderness that was almost whisper-soft.

One evening, a friend found him kneeling beside a child who had been restless with fever. Muller held a damp cloth against the little one's head and prayed so gently that the room felt warmer. When the friend asked later why he spent so much time on tasks others could handle, Muller replied, "Because love is shown most clearly in quiet service."

His life became a testimony that a servant heart is not built through grand sacrifice, but through small acts of kindness offered steadily, faithfully, and quietly.

***

A servant heart is one of the most beautiful qualities within a marriage. It transforms ordinary moments into opportunities to show love. When spouses choose to serve one another, they build trust, soften tension, and create an atmosphere of warmth and support. Service does not mean losing identity. It means choosing to bless, noticing needs, and willingly stepping into small acts of love.

A servant heart is often expressed in simple ways. Bringing a cup of water. Finishing a task so the other can rest. Offering comfort without being asked. These acts carry weight because they communicate care without demanding recognition.

Halfway into this truth, Mark 10:45 offers the example of Christ, who came "not to be served, but to serve." His life teaches that love grows strongest when expressed through humble service.

In marriage, serving one another builds unity. It turns daily routines into shared partnership. It reduces resentment by replacing self focus with compassion. When both spouses practice small acts of service, the home becomes a place where love is felt, not only spoken.

***

Embracing a servant heart in marriage strengthens the relationship in profound ways. Service is not a list of chores or obligations. It is a posture of love. It communicates, "I see you. I care about you. I want to support you." When this posture becomes part of daily life, the entire emotional atmosphere of the home changes.

A servant heart begins with noticing. It pays attention to signs of stress, fatigue, or discouragement. Instead of waiting to be asked, it steps forward willingly. Serving can be as simple as placing a warm drink beside your spouse, folding laundry when the other is overwhelmed, or offering a moment of rest during a busy day. These small choices make a large impact because they build a pattern of quiet consideration.

Service also guards the marriage from resentment. When both spouses give generously, no one feels alone in the responsibilities of daily life. Each act of service becomes a reminder that marriage is a partnership rather than a competition. Serving one another regularly creates emotional deposits that strengthen the relationship over time.

Another benefit is that service increases affection. When a spouse feels cared for in practical ways, their heart naturally softens. Service becomes a form of emotional communication, telling the other person that they are valued. These gestures become part of the couple's shared language of love.

A servant heart also requires humility. It means choosing to set aside personal convenience in order to bless the other. It asks both spouses to release pride and embrace compassion. When both partners practice this consistently, conflict decreases because each one prioritizes peace.

Finally, serving reflects the character of Christ. Scripture shows Him washing feet, feeding the hungry, and comforting the weary. Marriage becomes more spiritually grounded when spouses follow His example. A servant heart does not diminish the giver. It enriches both hearts and strengthens the unity of the home.

***

FROM HIS PERSPECTIVE

I used to think that serving my wife meant stepping in only during big moments or helping with major decisions. Over time I learned that the small things make the greatest difference. A friend once told me that he started asking God every morning, "Show me one way to serve my wife today." He said the answer was rarely dramatic. Sometimes it meant warming the car early on cold mornings. Sometimes it meant listening without checking his phone. Sometimes it meant cleaning the kitchen because he noticed she was tired.

He said those small choices transformed his marriage. His wife grew more open, more relaxed, and more affectionate because she felt supported in a consistent and meaningful way.

Hearing his experience challenged me. I began paying attention to simple opportunities to serve. Bringing her coffee. Taking something off her plate. Offering encouragement when the day has been heavy. I noticed how these choices soften her stress and draw us closer.

Serving her is not a duty I check off. It is a way of saying, "You matter to me." It strengthens my heart toward her and makes our home feel peaceful and united.

FROM HER PERSPECTIVE

I have learned that serving in marriage is much more than completing tasks. It is an attitude of care. It is choosing to notice when my husband seems overwhelmed and offering help before he asks. It is speaking gently when he looks discouraged. It is doing the small things that communicate, "You are not alone."

When he serves me in simple ways, I feel safer and more cherished. And when I serve him, I feel our connection deepen. Service softens misunderstandings. It changes the tone of our conversations. It reminds us that we are partners who support one another.

The more we serve with willingness and joy, the stronger our unity becomes. Service builds bridges between us, especially during difficult weeks. It helps us see each other not through frustration, but through love.

PRAYER

Lord, teach us to embrace a servant heart. Help us notice each other's needs and respond with love. Give us humility to bless one another without seeking recognition. Fill our home with small acts of kindness that strengthen our unity and reflect Your compassion. Shape our hearts to serve freely, joyfully, and consistently. Let our marriage honor You through every gesture of care. Amen.

CONVERSATION PROMPTS

1. When do you feel most supported by me in practical ways? Are there small acts of service that make your day feel lighter or your heart feel cared for? Help me understand what meaningful service looks like to you so I can love you more intentionally.

2. What areas of our daily life feel unbalanced or burdensome right now? How can we share those responsibilities with more compassion and partnership? Which habits could we adjust to create a more peaceful rhythm in our home?

CONNECTION PRACTICES

Choose one act of service today that your spouse usually handles. Complete it quietly, without announcing it. Later tonight, share one way your spouse served you this week in a way that brought comfort or lifted your burden.

30. Showing Love Through Small Acts

Now there was at Joppa a certain disciple named Tabitha,
which by interpretation is called Dorcas:
this woman was full of good works and almsdeeds.
Acts 9:36

The narrow streets of Joppa were unusually quiet that morning. A few early risers moved between stone houses, carrying baskets or drawing water, but their voices stayed low, as if something sacred or sorrowful had settled over the town. Inside one small upper room, several women sat gathered, their eyes red from weeping. They held garments in their hands, running their fingers along the seams as though touching the fabric kept a memory alive.

The room felt heavy with loss, but also strangely full. The air carried the scent of wool, oil, and tears. Every cloak, tunic, and robe in the room had a story. Each one had been sewn by a woman named Dorcas, known throughout Joppa for kindness that seemed to find its way into every corner of the community.

No one could forget her quiet generosity. Dorcas had no grand platform, no public speeches, no dramatic displays of faith. Yet her small acts of love had changed the lives of widows, children, and weary travelers. Her hands had stitched comfort into fabric and hope into hearts.

On that day when Peter was called to the home, the evidence of her love filled the room. Her small acts had become her legacy.

***

Dorcas teaches an unforgettable truth. Love expressed through small acts carries deep spiritual weight. Scripture describes her not by achievements or authority, but by kindness and steady generosity. The people of Joppa did not remember her for impressive speeches or displays. They remembered her for sewing clothes with her hands, meeting needs one stitch at a time.

In marriage, small acts of love build a foundation of tenderness. A gentle word, a small favor, a quiet sacrifice, or a moment of unexpected help sends a powerful message. These acts communicate, "You matter to me," and they strengthen emotional connection in ways that grand gestures cannot always reach.

Halfway through this truth, Acts 9:36 describes Dorcas as full of good works and charitable deeds. Her love was consistent, intentional, and quietly transformative.

When spouses practice small acts of love daily, their home becomes a place where affection grows naturally. The little things accumulate into a pattern of care, shaping the emotional rhythm of the marriage. Small acts build warmth, trust, and unity.

***

Showing love through small acts is one of the most powerful ways to strengthen a marriage. While grand expressions of affection have their place, it is the steady rhythm of small, thoughtful gestures that creates a lasting emotional bond. These gestures communicate love in a way that feels approachable, sincere, and deeply personal. They weave tenderness into daily life, turning ordinary moments into opportunities to bless one another.

Small acts often require attention more than effort. They begin with noticing. You see your spouse is tired and bring them a warm drink. You hear discouragement in their voice and offer a gentle moment of encouragement. You take on a task that they usually handle without being asked. These acts may seem insignificant, yet they carry tremendous emotional weight.

Small acts also build emotional safety. When a spouse consistently shows thoughtfulness, the other feels cherished and supported. The home becomes a refuge rather than a place of stress. Over time, these gestures reduce tension because they remind both partners that they are not alone in the responsibilities of life.

Another benefit is that small acts help prevent resentment. When each spouse takes the initiative to serve in little ways, the load feels lighter. The marriage becomes a partnership marked by shared care rather than silent expectations. Each small act becomes a deposit into the emotional bank of the relationship.

Small acts also soften conflict. A gentle gesture after tension shows humility and helps restore peace. It communicates that the relationship matters more than the disagreement. Even in seasons of stress, small acts can bridge emotional distance.

Finally, small acts reflect the character of Christ, who often extended love through quiet deeds of compassion. When couples imitate His gentleness, they bring spiritual depth into their relationship.

Small acts may look simple, but they build a marriage rich with tenderness, stability, and mutual affection.

***

FROM HIS PERSPECTIVE

I have learned that the small things often mean the most. When I surprised her with a favorite snack after a long day. When I filled her gas tank without mentioning it. When I took over a task she usually handles because I could tell she needed rest. I notice how her shoulders relax and her eyes soften.

The small acts do more than show love. They build trust. They tell her that she is not walking through life alone. The more intentional I am with these gestures, the deeper our connection grows. Small acts have power. They do not require planning. They require presence. They remind both of us that love grows strongest in the daily moments we choose to care.

FROM HER PERSPECTIVE

When I think about the moments that have strengthened our marriage, many of them are small and quiet. The morning he warmed the car so I would not step into the cold. The evening he folded a load of laundry because he could see I was worn down. The way he sometimes reaches for my hand without saying a word. These gestures feel like whispers of love that settle gently into my heart.

Small acts remind me that he pays attention. They also help me love him better. When I bring him a cup of coffee during a busy afternoon or slip a note into his pocket, I feel our bond deepen. These gestures do not erase challenges, but they soften them. They pull us closer when life feels heavy.

The small acts build a pattern of safety and affection. Each one says, "I am here with you." And that simple truth makes our marriage feel stronger, warmer, and more tender.

PRAYER

Lord, teach us to show love through small acts. Help us notice each other's needs and respond with kindness. Shape our hearts to give freely and cheerfully. Remind us that even simple gestures can carry Your compassion and bring warmth into our home. Let our daily interactions be filled with gentleness and generosity. Build a spirit of thoughtful love between us so our marriage becomes a place where care is felt in every season. Amen.

CONVERSATION PROMPTS

1. Which small acts of love mean the most to you? Are there gestures that make you feel especially cared for or supported? Help me understand the little things that speak love to your heart so I can practice them more intentionally.

2. Are there areas in our daily routine where small acts could make life feel lighter or more connected? What changes could we make that would help us serve each other in a gentler, more thoughtful way?

CONNECTION PRACTICES

Choose one small act of love today and offer it quietly. In the evening, share one small act your spouse did this week that brought comfort, encouragement, or joy.

31: Nurturing Emotional Affection

"A friend loveth at all times, and a brother is born for adversity."
Proverbs 17:17

The evening light was fading across the living room as the family settled into their usual end of day rhythm. Emeline had finished her homework and curled up with a blanket near the window. Paldy was sprawled across the rug with a half built Lego spaceship, humming quietly. The house felt peaceful, but he noticed something different when he walked in from work. His wife moved with her usual calm, yet her smile did not quite reach her eyes.

After the kids went to bed, he found her in the kitchen rinsing dishes slowly, lost in thought. He could tell something had weighed on her throughout the day. Instead of asking a quick question or offering a solution, he stepped close and touched her shoulder gently. She paused, surprised by the softness of the moment. He whispered, "Talk to me. I want to know how your heart is tonight."

That single invitation opened everything. She leaned against him and let the tears she had held in all day finally fall. No raised voices. No tension. Just a safe space created by emotional affection. His quiet presence became the comfort she needed.

That night taught them both that affection is not only physical. Sometimes it is the steady warmth that says, "Your heart is safe with me."

***

Emotional affection is one of the deepest forms of connection in marriage. It is the ability to notice the quiet changes in your spouse's mood, the unspoken signals that reveal how they are truly doing. Emotional affection communicates care before words are spoken. It shows that you are present not only with your actions, but with your attention.

This type of affection builds trust. When a spouse knows that their emotional world will be met with gentleness rather than criticism, they begin to open up more freely. Over time, emotional affection becomes a refuge within the home.

Halfway into this truth, Proverbs 17:17 reminds us that a friend loves at all times. In marriage, this means being present in both the joyful and the heavy moments, and showing tenderness in each one.

Emotional affection strengthens communication, reduces misunderstandings, and draws couples closer. It reminds both spouses that they are seen, supported, and valued. When emotional affection becomes a daily rhythm, the marriage becomes a place where both hearts can rest.

***

Nurturing emotional affection is essential for a healthy and secure marriage. Emotional affection is not dramatic or elaborate. It is expressed through quiet attention, gentle responses, and steady presence. When spouses learn to connect emotionally, the relationship grows deeper, becomes more resilient, and develops a warmth that sustains intimacy through every season.

Emotional affection begins with awareness. It requires paying attention to subtle cues such as tone, posture, or facial expressions. This awareness says, "I notice you. I care about what you feel even before you say it." It is a form of love that listens with the heart.

It also requires patience. Emotional affection grows slowly as trust builds. When spouses respond with calmness rather than frustration, vulnerability becomes easier. When soft words replace quick reactions, emotional closeness strengthens. Small moments of gentle curiosity create a safe place for sharing joys, fears, and struggles.

Another key aspect is empathy. Emotional affection asks spouses to imagine what the other might be feeling and respond with compassion instead of judgment. Empathy softens hard days and turns ordinary evenings into meaningful connection.

Emotional affection also shapes the home environment. It reduces defensiveness, increases tenderness, and prevents small misunderstandings from growing into larger conflicts. Couples who practice emotional affection experience fewer emotional barriers because the heart feels protected.

Finally, emotional affection brings spiritual depth. It mirrors the way God draws near to the brokenhearted and cares for the weary. When spouses show emotional affection, they imitate His gentleness, creating a marriage that reflects patience, kindness, and understanding.

A marriage rich in emotional affection does not avoid difficulties. Instead, it faces them with unity. Emotional affection becomes the steady warmth that keeps two hearts connected even in stressful seasons. Over time, it turns the home into a refuge where both spouses feel loved deeply and known fully.

FROM HIS PERSPECTIVE

I have learned that emotional affection is not about finding the perfect words. It is about being present in a way that invites my wife to open her heart. One evening, a friend told me how he began sitting beside his wife at the end of each day and saying nothing at first. He explained that he just wanted her to feel his presence before they talked. Over time, she began to share more because she felt safe.

His story made me notice how often I rush to fix things instead of offering stillness. Emotional affection asks me to slow down, look into her eyes, and ask gentle questions like, "How can I support you right now?" When I lean in with patience, I feel her relax. Our connection deepens. Emotional affection teaches me that closeness grows when I choose presence over pressure.

FROM HER PERSPECTIVE

I often find that emotional affection helps me feel grounded. When my husband notices the small changes in my voice or the expression on my face, I feel understood. Emotional affection tells me that my heart matters to him. It creates a space where I can share without fear of being dismissed or rushed.

When he listens quietly, when his tone softens, or when he simply reaches for my hand, the stress I carry begins to ease. Emotional affection helps me open up in ways that physical affection alone cannot. It deepens my trust and reminds me that our marriage is a partnership built not only on love, but on the comfort of being emotionally seen.

PRAYER

Lord, teach us to nurture emotional affection. Help us notice the quiet needs of one another and respond with patience and gentleness. Soften our hearts so that our home becomes a place where vulnerability is met with safety. Grant us empathy, wisdom, and tenderness as we care for each other's emotions. Strengthen our connection through Your love and guide us in becoming present, attentive, and compassionate partners. Amen.

CONVERSATION PROMPTS

1. What gestures or moments make you feel most emotionally cared for? Are there specific ways I can show more tenderness or awareness during difficult days? Help me understand the expressions of affection that speak most clearly to your heart.

2. Are there times when emotional affection feels harder to give or receive? What makes those moments challenging, and how can we gently support each other so that emotional closeness remains strong even on stressful days?

CONNECTION PRACTICES

Select one moment today to show emotional affection with intention. Offer a gentle touch, a kind word, or a quiet invitation to share feelings. Later, identify one instance this week when emotional affection from your spouse strengthened your heart.

32. Repairing Conflict Well

"If it be possible, as much as lieth
in you, live peaceably with all men."
Romans 12:18

The sun had just begun to set when a group of men approached David with tense expressions. Their voices were hushed, their steps hurried. Trouble had passed through the camp again. Two of David's most trusted followers had fallen into a sharp disagreement. It had started with a misunderstanding over resources and quickly grew into a heated argument that echoed through the tents. Both men were loyal to David, both committed to the cause, but their tempers had pushed them apart.

David listened carefully as each man explained his side. Neither wanted to be the one who yielded. Neither wanted to admit hurt or fear. Their words revealed more than frustration. They revealed wounded pride, fatigue, and the weight of long days spent in hiding.

David did not scold them. Instead, he looked at each man with a calm steadiness and spoke gently. He reminded them of their shared mission, their shared loyalty, and the God who had carried them this far. His words softened the tension. Slowly, the two men lowered their shoulders, then their voices, then their defenses.

That evening, reconciliation grew in the quiet space created by humility and patient listening. Their conflict did not destroy their bond. With wisdom and softness, it was repaired.

***

Conflict is unavoidable in marriage, but damage is not. How couples repair conflict determines the strength of their connection. When tension rises, emotions can overshadow understanding. Words can grow sharp. But when spouses learn to slow the moment, listen, and approach each other with gentleness, the conflict becomes an opportunity for deeper unity.

Repairing conflict well requires humility. It means acknowledging hurt feelings, not just facts. It means choosing to see the heart behind the words rather than reacting only to the tone. When both spouses soften, the atmosphere becomes safer, and reconciliation becomes possible.

Halfway into this truth, Romans 12:18 provides a guiding principle. "If it is possible, as far as it depends on you, live at peace with everyone." In marriage, this means doing your part to bring peace, even when the situation feels tense.

Repairing conflict well does not mean avoiding disagreement. It means approaching it with intention. When spouses pursue peace actively, their bond strengthens, trust grows, and their hearts remain connected even during difficult moments.

***

Repairing conflict well is essential for any marriage that aims to grow in unity and emotional safety. Conflict itself is not the enemy. Misunderstandings, unmet expectations, and stressful days are part of human life. What damages a marriage is unresolved conflict, lingering tension, or patterns of harsh responses. Repair happens when both spouses choose humility, gentleness, and a desire to understand rather than to win.

Repair begins with slowing down. When emotions are high, clarity disappears. Taking a moment to breathe or step back helps prevent hurtful reactions. Once calm returns, listening becomes possible. Listening without interrupting communicates value and gives space for the heart to speak.

Another part of repair is acknowledging feelings. Emotional wounds heal faster when each spouse feels understood. Phrases like "I can see why that hurt you" or "I understand why you felt unseen" build trust and reduce defensiveness. Validation does not mean agreement. It means compassion.

Repair also requires responsibility. Owning one's part in the conflict softens the other person. Simple, sincere apologies build bridges that defensiveness cannot. Apologies do not erase the issue, but they make the heart willing to move forward.

One of the most powerful aspects of repair is choosing unity over pride. When spouses prioritize the relationship above the argument, solutions come more easily. They approach the problem as a team rather than opponents.

Finally, forgiveness completes the repair. Forgiveness does not deny the hurt. It releases the tension so peace can return. When couples forgive quickly, they prevent resentment from taking root.

Repairing conflict well takes practice, but it builds a marriage marked by safety, tenderness, and deep connection.

FROM HIS PERSPECTIVE

I have learned that conflict does not damage our marriage as much as my reactions do. When I respond quickly or defensively, I escalate what could have been gentle. A close friend once told me that he and his wife would pause every time an argument began to rise. He said the pause did not solve everything, but it changed the tone of their conversations. Over time, that pause became a space where they caught their breath and softened.

His experience made me look at my own patterns. When I slow down, listen, and choose a calmer tone, I feel my wife ease. The argument becomes smaller. Repair becomes easier. I realize that my willingness to soften often invites her to relax too.

Repairing conflict well makes me feel closer to her. It reminds me that we are not fighting each other. We are fighting for each other. The faster I choose gentleness, the quicker we find peace again.

FROM HER PERSPECTIVE

I am learning that conflict does not mean something is wrong with us. It means we care enough to feel deeply. What matters most is how we return to each other afterward. When my husband stays present and listens, my heart calms. When he acknowledges my feelings, even without agreeing, I feel understood. That understanding makes it easier to lower my defenses.

I also see how my own reactions shape our connection. When I breathe before responding, or when I speak with softness rather than frustration, the tension fades sooner. Repairing conflict well helps me feel more connected, more supported, and more secure. It strengthens the bond between us in a way that smooth days never could.

PRAYER

Lord, help us repair conflict with humility and compassion. Teach us to listen with patience, speak with gentleness, and seek peace above pride. Strengthen our hearts with wisdom so that we respond rather than react. Heal the places where tension has lingered and restore tenderness in our home. Help us choose unity during difficult moments and guide our steps toward reconciliation. Fill our relationship with Your peace. Amen.

CONVERSATION PROMPTS

1. What do you need from me during conflict in order to feel safe, heard, and valued? Are there specific phrases or responses that help you feel understood when emotions rise?

2. Which part of conflict repair feels hardest for you: listening, apologizing, softening your tone, or forgiving? How can we support each other gently in those areas?

CONNECTION PRACTICES

Choose one step of conflict repair to practice this week. It could be pausing before responding, listening fully, or offering a sincere apology. At the end of the week, talk about how it strengthened your connection.

33. Pursuing Purity Together

"Wherewithal shall a young man cleanse his way?
by taking heed thereto according to thy word."
Psalm 119:9

The wooden floorboards of the small mission schoolhouse creaked softly as Elisabeth sat at her desk, reading Jim's latest letter. The world outside seemed ordinary enough, but the words she held carried a depth that made her hands tremble slightly. Jim wrote with honesty and conviction, sharing his dreams for ministry, his desire to honor God, and his deep affection for her. Yet woven into every page was a steady, disciplined commitment to purity that shaped their entire relationship.

During their courtship, they faced long seasons of waiting. Separation tested them. Their feelings were strong, and their future uncertain. But they shared a promise that whatever happened, they would honor God with their choices. Friends later recalled how Jim carried his convictions quietly but firmly. He refused to let emotions lead them where their faith could not follow.

Elisabeth once wrote that the strength of their love was built on self control, patience, and a shared desire to please God above all else. Their purity was not cold distance. It was warmth held with reverence. It was affection shaped by conviction. It was a love that grew deeper because it grew slower.

Their story endures because they pursued purity with courage and tenderness, trusting that God would honor their restraint with a greater intimacy in time.

***

Purity in marriage is not limited to physical boundaries. It is a constant choice to guard thoughts, intentions, and actions so that love remains honorable and secure. Purity protects the heart from distractions, hidden comparisons, or attitudes that weaken trust. It creates emotional clarity and strengthens spiritual unity.

Pursuing purity together means encouraging each other toward integrity. It involves open conversations, gentle accountability, and a shared desire to keep the marriage unclouded by habits that harm intimacy. Purity invites both spouses to love with intention rather than impulse.

Halfway into this truth, Psalm 119:9 asks a timeless question. "How can a young person stay on the path of purity?" The answer that follows is simple and steady. "By living according to Your word." Purity is not achieved through willpower alone. It is strengthened by drawing close to God.

When couples choose purity, they protect their hearts, honor one another, and build a foundation of trust that can withstand temptation and stress. Purity keeps love clean, safe, and deeply connected.

***

Pursuing purity together shapes a marriage with trust, safety, and emotional clarity. Purity is often misunderstood as a set of rules or restrictions, but in the context of marriage, purity is an active commitment to protect the relationship from anything that weakens intimacy. It is choosing thoughts, actions, and habits that strengthen unity rather than erode it.

Purity begins internally. It involves guarding the mind against comparisons, fantasies, or emotional attachments that do not belong in the marriage. It asks spouses to stay mindful of what they consume, whether through entertainment, media, or social interactions. A pure heart protects the marriage from unseen threats that often begin quietly.

Purity also involves transparency. When spouses speak honestly about struggles or vulnerabilities, they create a safe space for growth. Hiding creates distance, but openness builds trust. Couples who pursue purity together work as a team, supporting one another with grace and humility.

Another aspect of purity is emotional integrity. It means being careful with affection, attention, and conversation outside the marriage. Even seemingly harmless interactions can pull the heart in unhealthy directions if not approached with wisdom. Purity keeps emotional boundaries strong so that intimacy is reserved for the marriage alone.

Purity also nurtures tenderness. When spouses know they are protecting each other's hearts intentionally, affection grows deeper. The marriage becomes a place where both can relax, knowing they are valued completely.

Finally, pursuing purity invites God into the center of the relationship. Spiritual closeness strengthens purity because it aligns the heart with truth. Couples who pray together, read together, or seek God's guidance together find that purity becomes more natural. Temptation loses power when the heart is anchored.

Purity does not demand perfection. It invites commitment. It asks both spouses to walk with humility, honesty, and love as they protect their bond.

FROM HIS PERSPECTIVE

I have learned that purity in marriage is shaped by the choices I make long before temptation ever appears. It grows in the small, consistent decisions to guard my heart and protect the trust my wife places in me. When I keep my thoughts focused, my boundaries clear, and my attention centered on her, it strengthens our connection. Purity is not about restriction. It is about devotion. It is one of the ways I say, through quiet daily actions, "I choose you."

It keeps my heart steady, my intentions true, and our relationship safe.

FROM HER PERSPECTIVE

When I think about purity, I think about a moment early in our marriage that shaped me deeply. We had been invited to a gathering, and someone at the table made a comment that left me feeling suddenly insecure. It was small, but it touched an old wound from my past. I stayed quiet, unsure how to explain what I felt.

Later that evening, he noticed my silence and asked gently, "Are you all right" I hesitated, then shared the memory the comment had triggered. He listened without interruption, without brushing it aside. When I finished, he said quietly, "Your heart matters to me. I want you to feel protected with me."

That moment became a turning point. I realized purity was not only about guarding actions. It was about guarding each other's hearts. It was about honesty, tenderness, and choosing to protect the emotional places that feel most vulnerable.

Since then, I have learned to guard my own heart for him too—my thoughts, my interactions, my emotional availability. Pursuing purity together makes our love feel intentional and safe. It strengthens our trust, deepens our unity, and reminds me that we are building something sacred and wholehearted.

PRAYER

Lord, teach us to pursue purity together with humility and devotion. Guard our hearts from distractions that weaken intimacy. Strengthen our desire to honor one another and keep our love protected. Fill our marriage with trust, clarity, and spiritual strength. Help us choose integrity in small moments and truth in hidden places. May purity become a source of peace and unity in our home. Amen.

CONVERSATION PROMPTS

1. What helps you feel most protected and valued in our marriage? Are there boundaries or habits that help strengthen your sense of emotional and spiritual purity?

2. Are there areas where purity feels more difficult to maintain? How can we support each other gently and without judgment as we grow in this together?

CONNECTION PRACTICES

Choose one way to protect your marriage this week. It could be setting a boundary, offering extra transparency, or removing a small distraction. Share the impact together at the end of the week.

34. Building a Marriage of Purpose

"And found a certain Jew named Aquila, born in Pontus,
lately come from Italy, with his wife Priscilla;
(because that Claudius had commanded all Jews
to depart from Rome:) and came unto them.
And because he was of the same craft, he abode with them,
and wrought: for by their occupation they were tentmakers."
Acts 18:2–3

The marketplace in Corinth was already alive when the sun rose above the rooftops. Merchants called from their stalls, travelers brushed past one another, and the smell of baked bread drifted through the narrow streets. Near the edge of the market, a small workshop stood open, its doorway warm with lamplight. Inside, two figures worked side by side, weaving leather cords and shaping tent frames with steady hands.

Aquila adjusted a beam while Priscilla stitched along the edge of a tent sheet. Their movements were practiced, almost rhythmic. They did not need many words. Years of shared work had formed a quiet harmony between them. Anyone passing by could sense that their partnership was not only in labor, but in heart and purpose.

Their lives had not been simple. They had been forced to leave Rome. They had rebuilt their trade in Corinth. They had faced uncertainty more than once. Yet instead of letting hardship divide them, it knit them together. Their workshop became more than a place of business. It became a meeting ground for weary believers, travelers seeking guidance, and eventually Paul himself.

Aquila and Priscilla were not known for dramatic miracles. They were known for a marriage shaped by shared purpose, steady faith, and a willingness to serve God together wherever He led.

***

Aquila and Priscilla reveal the beauty of a marriage driven by shared purpose. Their story in Acts shows a couple who worked together, traveled together, taught together, and supported the early church as a team. They were not perfect, but they lived with unity of direction. Their faith shaped their decisions, their home, and their daily work.

Purpose in marriage does not mean identical roles. It means moving in the same direction. It is choosing to see your life as a shared calling rather than two separate paths. Purpose gives meaning to challenges and brings strength to ordinary days.

Halfway into this truth, Acts 18:2–3 shows them living out their purpose through simple work. They welcomed Paul into their trade and later into their home. Their purpose was not about spotlight moments. It was about faithfulness.

A marriage built on purpose offers stability, direction, and hope. It keeps couples united during change and anchored in seasons of stress. When spouses seek God together and pursue a shared vision, their marriage becomes a partnership that reflects God's design.

***

Building a marriage of purpose invites couples to live with greater unity, direction, and intentionality. Purpose is not simply a list of accomplishments or a set of goals. It is the deeper understanding that God has brought two people together for reasons that reach beyond daily tasks. A purposeful marriage looks at both strengths and weaknesses and asks, "How can we honor God together in our home, in our work, and in our relationships"

Purpose creates unity. When couples define what matters most to them, decisions become clearer. They can filter opportunities, habits, and commitments through a shared vision. This reduces conflict because both spouses know they are working toward the same values.

Purpose also deepens intimacy. When spouses share spiritual goals, they draw one another closer. Whether serving in ministry, raising children with intention, or supporting one another's callings, purpose helps each spouse feel appreciated and understood. They become partners in something meaningful rather than simply sharing a house.

Purpose brings meaning to challenges. When difficulties come, purpose reminds couples that hardships can strengthen them. Like Aquila and Priscilla, who faced relocation and uncertainty, couples with purpose learn to grow closer during adversity. They see trials as opportunities to trust God together.

Purpose shapes the home environment. A purposeful home has rhythms of prayer, encouragement, and thoughtful conversation. It becomes a refuge that fosters growth and peace.

Finally, purpose brings spiritual depth. When couples seek God's guidance regularly, they align their desires with His heart. This unity brings clarity and strength to the marriage. A purposeful marriage becomes a testimony to God's faithfulness as both spouses walk forward with clarity, love, and shared mission.

A marriage of purpose does not happen instantly. It grows through daily choices, honest conversations, and a desire to honor God together. Over time, purpose becomes the steady foundation that guides the relationship through every season.

***

FROM HIS PERSPECTIVE

I think often about how purpose changes the way a man approaches marriage. A friend once told me that he and his wife sat down one evening and talked for the first time about what they believed God wanted for their relationship. He said that conversation changed everything. Instead of moving through life as two individuals trying to manage responsibilities, they began seeing their marriage as a team carrying the same vision.

His words made something shift within me. When I look at my wife and ask what God might want us to build together, I feel a deeper love for her. I feel more responsible for stewarding our relationship with care. Purpose reminds me that our marriage is not accidental. It is intentional. It is meaningful. And it shapes how I choose to show up for her every day.

When we move toward the same goals, I feel connected not only to her heart, but also to God's direction for us. Purpose gives our love a deeper root.

FROM HER PERSPECTIVE

When I think of purpose in marriage, I think of partnership. I feel closest to my husband when we are working toward something together, whether it is parenting with intention, supporting one another's dreams, or serving others in small ways. Purpose helps me see the beauty in our differences. It reminds me that God brought us together because we strengthen one another.

When we talk about our goals or pray about our decisions, I feel more secure. I feel like we are moving with unity instead of drifting. Purpose protects us from growing distant because it invites us to stay connected in both heart and direction. It makes our home feel grounded and hopeful.

PRAYER

Lord, show us the purpose You have for our marriage. Help us move in unity, listen for Your guidance, and support one another with grace. Strengthen our partnership so our home becomes a place where Your love is reflected. Give us clarity in decisions, patience in challenges, and joy in the work You call us to share. Teach us to build a marriage centered on Your will. Amen.

CONVERSATION PROMPTS

1. What parts of our life feel most purposeful to you, and which areas feel unclear? How can we pursue God's direction together in a meaningful way?

2. How can we better support each other's individual callings while still moving together with unity as a couple? What practical steps would help us feel more aligned?

CONNECTION PRACTICES

Choose one shared purpose to focus on this week, such as prayer, serving someone in need, or encouraging a friend. Do it together and reflect on how it strengthened your unity.

35. When Storms Come Unexpectedly

When thou passest through the waters, I will be with thee;
and through the rivers, they shall not overflow thee:
when thou walkest through the fire, thou shalt not be burned;
neither shall the flame kindle upon thee.
Isaiah 43:2

The storm warnings had mentioned rain, but no one expected the sky to darken as suddenly as it did that afternoon. Emeline was working on a school project at the dining table, and Paldy was on the floor building a tower of wooden blocks. The air shifted in a strange way, the kind that makes everyone pause. Within minutes, the wind picked up and the first heavy drops of rain struck the windows.

She looked up just as the lights flickered once, then twice, and finally went out. The room settled into an eerie quiet. The children drew closer, unsure but trying to be brave. He checked the weather report again, realizing the storm was stronger than expected. Branches outside began tapping against the siding, and thunder rolled closer.

When the wind howled loudly near the back door, she felt a knot forming in her stomach. He noticed the fear in her eyes and stepped beside her, placing a steady hand on her arm.

"We are here together," he said quietly so the kids could hear it too.

Something softened inside her. They gathered blankets, lit candles, and waited out the storm as a family. The wind raged outside, but the closeness inside turned fear into calm. That evening reminded them that storms do not break a family when they face them together.

***

Unexpected storms come into every marriage. Sometimes they arrive in the form of financial pressure, emotional strain, health concerns, or sudden changes in life. These storms shake routines, test patience, and challenge the sense of security. When pressure rises unexpectedly, couples can feel overwhelmed before they have a moment to prepare.

God offers steady assurance in these moments. Halfway into the promise found in Isaiah 43:2, He says that when you pass through deep waters, He will be with you. This comfort does not promise a life without storms, but it promises His presence in the middle of them.

Facing storms as a couple requires unity rather than isolation. It means sharing fears honestly and seeking comfort in one another instead of withdrawing. When couples pause, breathe, and approach the challenge side by side, they discover strength they did not know they had.

Unexpected storms do not have to shatter peace. With God's presence and a unified posture, storms become moments that draw couples closer and deepen trust.

***

When storms come unexpectedly, a marriage can feel shaken. Stress rises quickly, communication becomes strained, and fears surface that usually stay hidden. Yet these storms also hold the potential to strengthen the marriage in profound ways when handled with unity and tenderness.

Storms reveal vulnerabilities. They expose what feels fragile and highlight where support is most needed. Instead of ignoring these emotions, couples grow stronger when they acknowledge them openly. Saying, "I am scared," or "I do not know what to do," becomes a doorway to deeper closeness when the other responds with patience rather than pressure.

Storms also invite teamwork. When spouses step toward each other instead of away from each other, the burden becomes lighter. Facing challenges as partners rather than individuals helps prevent isolation. Unity allows each spouse to lean on the other in areas where they feel weak.

Another key to navigating storms is gentleness. Stress can make tempers shorter and words sharper. Choosing soft words and calm tones protects the relationship from damage during difficult moments. Gentleness becomes a form of shelter.

Faith anchors the couple. Returning to Scripture, prayer, and moments of shared quiet brings stability. When both partners seek God together, fear loses its grip. Spiritual unity becomes a refuge, much like a safe room within the storm.

Storms also bring opportunities for growth. They reveal strengths, deepen reliance on God, and build resilience. Couples often look back and realize the storm that once frightened them became a turning point in their intimacy.

A marriage grows stronger not because storms never come, but because the couple chooses to face them side by side with love, humility, and faith. Even in the fiercest season, God's presence offers comfort, and unity creates strength.

***

FROM HIS PERSPECTIVE

I have learned that storms tend to draw out the part of me that wants to appear strong at all times. When something unexpected hits, my instinct is to stay controlled, fix the problem quickly, and hide any fear or uncertainty. For a long time, I believed that protecting her meant never showing weakness. I thought steadiness meant silence. But I have come to understand that this kind of strength can create distance rather than comfort.

What truly helps her is not a perfect plan or an unshakable expression. What helps her is presence. She does not need me to have every answer. She needs to know that I am here, fully engaged, willing to walk through the difficulty with her rather than ahead of her or apart from her. When I slow down, breathe, and let her see that I feel the weight of the moment too, it deepens our connection instead of weakening it.

I have also realized that sharing the emotional load is not a sign of weakness. Admitting, "This is heavy for me too," creates space for honest partnership. It invites her into the process instead of pushing her to the sidelines. Storms feel less overwhelming when we face them together.

Now, when challenges rise, I try to be steady without shutting down. I reach for her hand, ask how she is feeling, and pay attention to what her heart needs. Choosing unity in the storm has become one of the clearest ways I can love her well.

FROM HER PERSPECTIVE

I used to think that storms meant something was wrong with our marriage. Now I see that storms reveal how much we need one another. When unexpected pressures come, my emotions rise quickly. Fear can make me tense or withdrawn. But when he steps close, listens, and reminds me we are not alone, peace begins to settle again.

I have learned that sharing my fears does not burden him. It helps us face the storm as one. When we pray together or simply sit with honesty, the pressure eases. Storms do not separate us. They pull us closer when we choose unity and let God meet us in the middle of the chaos.

PRAYER

Lord, be our strength when storms come unexpectedly. Help us face challenges with unity, gentleness, and steady faith. Calm the fears that rise quickly and guide our hearts to trust Your presence. Teach us to support one another with patience and compassion. Let our marriage grow stronger through every storm, grounded in Your peace and anchored in Your love. Amen.

CONVERSATION PROMPTS

1. What storms or pressures feel closest to you right now? Are there fears or worries you have not yet shared with me that I can help carry?

2. When unexpected challenges arise, what helps you feel supported rather than overwhelmed? How can I respond to you in a way that makes the storm feel more manageable?

CONNECTION PRACTICES

Choose one storm you are facing this week and talk through it as a team. Pray together, plan together, and remind each other that you are not alone.

36. Renewing Your Commitment Daily

They are new every morning: great is thy faithfulness.
Lamentations 3:23

It happened during a quiet Saturday morning, the kind where sunlight warmed the kitchen tile and the sound of the coffeemaker filled the silence. Marcus sat at the table scrolling through emails while Hannah moved around the kitchen preparing breakfast. They spoke politely but not intimately. The ease they once shared felt replaced by a careful distance neither fully acknowledged.

When she reached for a mug in the cabinet, her hand brushed against his old travel thermos. She paused, remembering the mornings when he used to fill it for her before her commute, leaving a small note tucked beneath the lid. It had been years since he had done that. Not because he loved her less, but because life had become crowded with responsibilities that slowly pushed out the little gestures that once knit them together.

She set the thermos on the counter and asked quietly, "Do you remember when you used to make my coffee before I left for work?" The question was gentle, but it stirred something in him. He looked up, realizing how far the small habits had drifted.

Without speaking, he stood and began making her coffee. When he handed her the mug, she smiled in a way he had not seen in a long time.

It was simple. Unremarkable. But it was a beginning. A small renewal in the quiet space of an ordinary morning.

***

Commitment in marriage is not sustained by a single promise made on one beautiful day. It is strengthened through small, daily decisions that reinforce love and connection. Over time, distractions, exhaustion, and routine can cause commitment to feel assumed rather than nurtured. When that happens, emotional closeness begins to thin.

Daily renewal means choosing your spouse again and again in simple, consistent ways. It means being intentional rather than drifting. It means remembering that love grows strongest when it is fed regularly with patience, attention, and tenderness.

Halfway into this truth, Lamentations 3:23 speaks a comforting reminder. God's mercies are new every morning. His renewal is continual, not occasional. This rhythm becomes a model for marriage, inviting couples to approach each day with a fresh commitment to kindness and connection.

Daily renewal restores warmth, deepens trust, and prevents hearts from slowly drifting apart. It keeps marriages from fading under the weight of routine.

***

Renewing commitment daily is one of the most transformative habits in a marriage. Commitment is not only the promise made at the altar. It is the steady choice to love faithfully in the ordinary moments that follow. When couples intentionally renew their commitment, they protect their relationship from drifting into emotional distance or silent resignation.

Daily renewal begins with presence. Couples who stay present with one another notice small changes, understand emotional needs, and respond before disconnection grows. Presence communicates value. It says, "You matter today just as much as you did when we first loved each other."

Another part of renewal is consistency. Small habits such as checking in during the day, offering a warm greeting, or ending the evening with affection create rhythms of connection. These habits seem simple, but they carry significant emotional weight.

Renewal also involves gratitude. When spouses express appreciation regularly, their hearts soften. Gratitude shifts focus from frustrations to blessings. It reminds couples of what is good, faithful, and worth nurturing.

Another essential piece is vulnerability. Renewing commitment daily requires honesty about feelings, fears, and desires. When spouses share openly, they deepen intimacy and prevent unspoken tension from taking root.

Forgiveness is also central. Daily renewal means choosing grace when miscommunication happens. It means letting go of small irritations before they grow into larger wounds. Forgiveness allows commitment to remain steady and warm.

Finally, daily renewal aligns the marriage with God's rhythm. Just as His mercies are renewed every morning, couples can choose to renew their tenderness, patience, and devotion each day. This keeps the marriage from stagnating and fills it with fresh hope.

A marriage strengthened by daily renewal becomes resilient, tender, and deeply connected. It grows through seasons rather than weakening in them.

***

FROM HIS PERSPECTIVE

I have learned that commitment cannot be something I set and forget. It needs attention every single day. A friend once told me that he began starting each morning by asking himself one question. "How can I love my wife well today" He said it shifted everything. He stopped waiting for big moments and started noticing small ones. A gentle word. A thoughtful gesture. A moment to help before being asked.

His story made me think about my own habits. When I intentionally choose her each day, something changes in our connection. She feels seen. I feel steady. Our conversations flow with more ease. Even on stressful days, the simple act of renewing my commitment softens the atmosphere. Daily choices matter more than I ever realized.

FROM HER PERSPECTIVE

Renewing my commitment daily has taught me that love grows strongest through consistency. It is easy to say I am committed, but daily renewal requires attention. It means offering kindness even when tired, listening even when distracted, and choosing to show affection even when the day feels heavy. When he does the same for me, I feel deeply valued. These daily choices strengthen my trust and bring peace into our home. Renewed commitment keeps us close, steady, and connected.

PRAYER

Lord, teach us to renew our commitment each day with tenderness and intention. Help us choose each other with fresh love every morning. Strengthen our unity, deepen our affection, and guide us to care for one another with consistency and grace. Give us wisdom to notice small needs and courage to speak gently. Let daily renewal become the rhythm that protects our marriage and reflects Your faithful love. Amen.

CONVERSATION PROMPTS

1. When do you feel most chosen by me in our daily life? Are there small gestures, words, or moments that help you feel secure and valued? How can I make those moments a more consistent part of our rhythm?

2. Are there areas where our commitment feels stretched or overlooked in busy seasons? What simple changes could help us stay emotionally close and steady each day? How can we support each other with kindness when stress begins to rise?

CONNECTION PRACTICES

Choose one small way to renew your commitment today. It might be a warm note, a thoughtful gesture, or an intentional moment of affection. In the evening, share how it strengthened your connection.

37. Seeing Each Other Through God's Eyes

The LORD said unto Samuel, Look not on his countenance,
or on the height of his stature; because I have refused him:
for the LORD seeth not as man seeth.
1 Samuel 16:7

It happened one evening after the kids were finally in bed. The house had that quiet hum it gets when everything is settled, but inside me, there was anything but quiet. I sat at the dining table pretending to finish an outline for our next chapter, but my mind kept circling a comment Emeline had made earlier that afternoon. It was small, probably not even meant the way I heard it, yet it struck a tender place I did not realize was unguarded.

She came into the room a few minutes later and sat across from me. "You are quiet," she said gently. Normally I would brush it off, but something in her tone invited honesty. I told her I felt discouraged and unsure about some things I had been carrying. She stayed still, listening in that calm way she has when she senses something deeper beneath the words.

What surprised me most was what she said next. "When I look at you, I see the man God is shaping, not the man who doubts himself." Her voice was soft, but her words settled into me with unexpected strength.

In that moment, I realized how often we forget to see each other through God's eyes. Her gentle reminder felt like light entering a dim room, lifting weight I had unknowingly placed on my own shoulders.

***

Seeing your spouse through God's eyes means looking deeper than moods, mistakes, or shortcomings. It means recognizing the work God is doing in them even when their growth feels slow or hidden. Human eyesight often stops at the surface. We see only the frustration of the moment or the habit that has not yet changed. But God sees the heart, the potential, and the coming fruit.

Halfway into this truth, 1 Samuel 16:7 tells us that humans look at outward appearance, but God looks at the heart. This perspective changes everything in marriage. It softens reactions, increases patience, and inspires prayer rather than criticism.

Seeing your spouse through God's eyes invites you to look for the good He planted within them. It means paying attention to character, intentions, and small signs of growth. It creates a lens of compassion and encourages unity instead of tension.

When couples learn to view one another this way, their conversations become kinder, their respect deepens, and their hearts draw closer.

***

Seeing each other through God's eyes reshapes the emotional and spiritual tone of a marriage. It is easy to focus on each other's weaknesses, especially during stressful seasons. Tiredness, misunderstandings, and daily pressures highlight imperfections. But when spouses intentionally shift their perspective, choosing to see through

God's lens, the relationship becomes filled with compassion and patience.

God sees potential long before it is visible. He sees growth beneath the surface and strength that is forming slowly. When spouses adopt this perspective, they learn to speak words that encourage rather than discourage. They begin to affirm qualities that may be small but are real. This affirmation builds confidence and courage within the marriage.

Another aspect of seeing through God's eyes is understanding that your spouse is a work in progress, just as you are. This removes unrealistic expectations. It helps couples approach each other with humility rather than frustration. Instead of reacting to flaws, they respond with grace.

Seeing your spouse through God's perspective also deepens affection. When you look for the good in your partner, your heart softens. You begin to notice virtues you once overlooked. You appreciate effort rather than demanding perfection. This shapes the marriage with warmth and tenderness.

Prayer also becomes a significant part of this shift. Asking God to help you see your spouse the way He does brings clarity. It invites the Holy Spirit to soften your heart and guide your thoughts. Over time, this practice creates emotional maturity and spiritual unity.

Finally, adopting God's perspective strengthens resilience. When conflict arises, couples who see each other with grace are quicker to repair. When disappointment comes, they encourage each other rather than withdraw. When challenges grow, they stand together rather than criticize.

Seeing each other through God's eyes is not a single moment of insight. It is a daily choice to view your spouse with compassion, hope, and respect. Over time, this choice transforms the marriage into a safe and loving partnership.

FROM HIS PERSPECTIVE

When Emeline once told me she saw the man God was shaping, something inside me steadied. I realized how much I needed her faith in moments when my own felt thin. Seeing each other through God's eyes does not ignore flaws. It simply acknowledges that God is not finished. When I look at her this way, I notice her strength, her patience, and the steady tenderness she offers even when tired. It changes the way I speak to her. It changes the way I listen. It makes me grateful.

FROM HER PERSPECTIVE

There are moments when I catch myself focusing on small frustrations and forgetting the deeper truth. When I pause and ask God to help me see Emmett as He does, I notice the steadiness in him, the love he carries quietly, and the way he tries even when he doubts himself. Seeing him this way softens my heart. It brings tenderness into our conversations and helps me love him with more patience and faith.

PRAYER

Lord, help us see each other through Your eyes. Teach us to notice the good You are forming, to speak with gentleness, and to extend grace willingly. Remove hurried judgments and soften the places where frustration tries to settle. Let our hearts reflect Your compassion so our marriage becomes a place where hope and encouragement grow daily. Amen.

CONVERSATION PROMPTS

1. What qualities in you do you wish I noticed more often? How can I become better at seeing the growth and potential God is shaping in you, especially during difficult seasons?

2. When do you feel most understood and seen by me? Are there ways I can respond, listen, or encourage that help you feel valued the way God values you?

CONNECTION PRACTICES

Choose one moment today to speak a sincere affirmation over your spouse, naming something God is growing in them. End the day by sharing one way you saw God's grace in each other.

38. Choosing Grace When Flaws Feel Bigger

Forbearing one another, and forgiving one another,
if any man have a quarrel against any:
even as Christ forgave you, so also do ye.

Colossians 3:13

During one of their early research seasons in Paris, Pierre and Marie Curie found themselves working in a drafty, makeshift laboratory that barely kept out the cold. Their long hours were spent bending over crude equipment, stirring chemicals, and carrying heavy containers of ore. Progress was painfully slow. Mistakes were common. Fatigue crept into every corner of their days. Their shared dream of discovery kept them going, but the strain pressed against their marriage in subtle ways.

One afternoon, after a series of failed measurements, Marie grew discouraged. The disappointment slipped into her words before she could stop it. Pierre turned at the sound of her frustration, seeing more than irritation. He saw the exhaustion etched across her face. Instead of reacting sharply, he stepped beside her and examined the instrument causing the trouble. He gently adjusted a single component and said quietly, "We will begin again."

She later described this moment as one that revealed the depth of their partnership. Pierre did not judge her fatigue or take offense at her tone. He understood the pressure weighing on both of them and responded with patience that steadied her spirit.

Their marriage endured not because they avoided strain, but because they offered grace when flaws felt magnified by difficulty.

***

Flaws often appear larger during seasons of pressure. Stress, disappointment, or exhaustion can make minor frustrations feel overwhelming. In marriage, moments like these can build unnecessary tension if spouses respond quickly rather than compassionately. Choosing grace allows couples to see beyond the moment and remember the heart behind the struggle.

Grace listens before reacting. It pauses. It looks for the reason beneath the tone. Instead of focusing on the flaw, grace pays attention to the weight the other person is carrying. This shift brings understanding and softens the atmosphere.

Halfway into this truth, Colossians 3:13 calls believers to bear with one another and to forgive as the Lord forgave. The verse encourages patience not as weakness but as a reflection of God's character. When couples practice grace, they bring His gentleness into their home.

Grace does not erase responsibility or avoid change. Instead, it keeps conflict from becoming destructive. It offers room to breathe and space to repair. In marriage, this choice creates safety, tenderness, and deeper trust.

***

Choosing grace when flaws feel bigger is essential to maintaining emotional closeness in marriage. Stress often magnifies imperfections, making little habits seem sharper and normal misunderstandings feel heavier. Without grace, the relationship becomes vulnerable to misinterpretation and distance. With grace, even difficult days can become opportunities for renewed tenderness.

Grace begins by seeing the whole person rather than the single moment. Every spouse carries a history of effort, affection, sacrifice, and growth. Remembering these truths helps reduce frustration. When couples view each other through the lens of shared years rather than the irritation of the hour, compassion naturally rises.

Another facet of grace is recognizing that pressure affects people differently. One spouse may grow quiet, while the other becomes more expressive. One may withdraw, while the other searches for connection. Instead of assuming intention, grace responds with curiosity and softness.

Grace also protects communication. When emotions are high, reactions often come quickly and harshly. Choosing a slower, gentler response prevents small issues from escalating. It signals that the relationship is more important than the momentary flaw.

Forgiveness is a vital component of grace. Letting go of minor failures creates emotional breathing room for both partners. When forgiveness is offered promptly, small offenses do not gather into larger barriers.

Grace is not passive. It is active love. It chooses understanding even when frustration feels justified. It chooses humility when pride wants to win. It chooses peace when tension threatens connection.

Finally, grace invites God into the relationship. His compassion teaches couples how to soften, how to wait, and how to respond with wisdom. As spouses practice grace, their marriage becomes a place of safety and restoration, where flaws do not dominate and love continues to deepen.

FROM HIS PERSPECTIVE

I have learned that my reactions shape the atmosphere of our home more than I once realized. When I am tired or stressed, I tend to notice flaws quickly. A small comment, a slight change in tone, or a simple oversight can feel larger than it should. But when I step back and choose grace, I see her differently. I remember her long days, her endless efforts for our family, and the tenderness she carries even in fatigue.

There was an evening when we were both stretched thin. She snapped at something minor, and my first instinct was to match the sharpness. Instead, I paused and looked at her more carefully. I saw the exhaustion in her eyes and the weight she had been holding alone. The irritation dissolved instantly. Grace made space for understanding.

When I respond with grace, our connection stays intact. When she offers me grace, I feel safe enough to admit my weakness instead of hiding it. Grace is not a soft escape. It is strength that protects our marriage from unnecessary wounds. It keeps us close, steady, and willing to try again.

FROM HER PERSPECTIVE

There are days when my flaws feel louder. I feel stretched thin, and my tone shifts before I realize it. When he responds with frustration, the distance grows quickly. But when he answers my sharp edges with gentleness, everything softens. I feel seen rather than judged. That kind of grace reminds me that I am loved, even in my imperfect moments.

I am learning to offer the same grace to him. Stress affects him differently. He grows quieter, sometimes withdrawn, and I used to interpret that as disinterest. Now I see the truth. He is trying to manage pressure in the only way he knows, and he needs space and kindness, not assumption.

Grace changes our marriage. It reminds me to slow down, breathe, and choose understanding over criticism. It helps me let go of small irritations and see the heart behind his actions. Grace teaches me that we are both growing, both trying, both human.

And when we both choose it, even flawed days become days of tenderness.

PRAYER

Lord, teach us to offer grace quickly and generously. Help us see each other's hearts rather than reacting to the surface of a difficult moment. Calm our frustrations and guide us to respond with compassion when flaws feel larger than they truly are. Shape our marriage into a place where understanding replaces irritation and forgiveness flows freely. Strengthen us to love with patience, humility, and gentleness. Let grace settle into our home like a steady peace that protects our connection. Amen.

CONVERSATION PROMPTS

1. When stress rises, what helps you feel understood rather than judged? Are there specific gestures, tones, or approaches that make it easier for you to open up instead of becoming defensive? I want to understand how to support you with greater sensitivity during moments when flaws feel magnified and your emotions are tender.

2. What makes it difficult for you to offer grace to me when I fall short? Are there patterns, memories, or fears that affect how you respond to my imperfections? How can we work together to create an atmosphere that encourages grace rather than quick frustration when our humanity shows?

CONNECTION PRACTICES

Choose one moment this week to respond with grace where irritation might normally surface. It could be a forgotten task, a tired tone, or a miscommunication. Pause, breathe, and offer softness instead of reaction. In the evening, talk gently about how this choice affected the atmosphere of your relationship and whether it helped reduce tension. End by expressing one word of appreciation for each other to reinforce the bond created by grace.

39. Standing Together When One Is Weary

"Moses hands were heavy; and they took a stone,
and put it under him, and he sat thereon;
and Aaron and Hur stayed up his hands,
the one on the one side, and the other on the other side;
and his hands were steady until the going down of the sun."
Exodus 17:12

The sun beat down over the valley as the battle against the Amalekites raged below. Moses stood on the hill overlooking the conflict, staff raised high. As long as his hands remained lifted, Israel prevailed. But the day grew long, and the weight of the staff pressed heavily against his strength. His arms trembled. His shoulders burned. With every moment of weakness, the tide of the battle shifted.

Aaron noticed the strain first. He saw Moses struggling to keep the staff lifted, saw the exhaustion seeping through his posture. Without hesitation, Aaron stepped beside him and placed his hand on Moses' elbow. On the other side, Hur moved close and did the same. They found a stone, helped Moses sit, and stood steady on each side, holding his hands high when he no longer could.

The battle turned again, but this time Moses did not stand alone. His strength had reached its limit, yet the support of those beside him kept the victory within reach.

This moment was more than a story of war. It was a picture of what happens when one person grows weary and another steps in with strength, presence, and unwavering support. Their unity won what individual strength could not.

***

Weariness comes to every marriage. Sometimes one spouse carries a burden that becomes too heavy to manage alone. Fatigue settles into their voice, their posture, or their spirit. These moments do not reflect weakness of character, but the limits of being human. Scripture gives a powerful image of this in Exodus 17:12. Moses' strength failed, but the battle was not lost because he had support at his side.

In marriage, one spouse often grows weary before the other. When this happens, unity becomes the source of strength. Stepping in for one another is not about fixing or rescuing. It is about standing close, offering presence, and carrying the weight together.

The verse teaches that victory is not always found in personal endurance. Sometimes it comes through shared strength. When spouses respond to each other's weariness with patience and support, pressure lessens. Hearts steady. Hope returns.

Standing together in weariness strengthens trust, deepens intimacy, and reflects the compassion of God.

***

Standing together when one spouse is weary is a central expression of covenant love. Marriage does not promise equal strength at all times. Instead, it offers a place where weakness can be met with tenderness and where burdens can be carried by two instead of one.

When one spouse is weary, the atmosphere of the home shifts. Tasks feel heavier. Emotions sit closer to the surface. Discouragement can creep in quietly. Without support, the weary spouse may feel isolated or misunderstood. But when couples commit to noticing signs of fatigue, the relationship becomes a refuge.

Support begins with attentiveness. Sometimes weariness shows up in small ways: slower responses, quieter conversations, or shorter patience. Instead of expecting the same level of energy, support invites compassion. It asks gentle questions and listens without pressure.

Another part of standing together is practical help. Whether it is taking over a responsibility, providing time for rest, or offering a comforting presence, practical support eases emotional strain. Small acts create significant relief.

Emotional support is equally important. Words of encouragement can restore strength. Affirming the effort your spouse has poured out reminds them that they are not alone. This emotional reinforcement rebuilds confidence.

Patience plays a vital role. Weariness does not disappear quickly. Offering space for recovery without judgment fosters trust. Couples who practice patience avoid turning fatigue into conflict.

Prayer strengthens this unity. When spouses bring each other's weariness before God, they find renewed peace. Shared prayer deepens spiritual connection and anchors the marriage in grace.

Standing together in times of weakness does not diminish individual responsibility. Instead, it honors the truth that God designed marriage to function as a partnership. When one is weary, the other becomes a source of stability. When the roles reverse, the support continues.

A marriage shaped by this rhythm becomes resilient, tender, and deeply connected. It mirrors the moment on the hill when victory came not through solitary strength, but through unity.

***

FROM HIS PERSPECTIVE

There are days when she carries more than she lets on. I see it in the way she folds laundry slower than usual, or how her smile does not hold as long. In the past, I used to miss these signs because I was consumed with my own work. But I am learning to pay attention, to notice the quiet signals that she is growing weary. When I step beside her, even in simple ways like finishing tasks or listening without interruption, I feel our bond strengthen.

There have been moments when my own strength has run thin, moments when discouragement settled heavier than I expected. She has stepped beside me with the same steady presence. Her support does not erase the difficulty, but it keeps me from feeling alone. When she offers words that remind me who I am and whose I am, something inside me steadies.

Standing together when one is weary is not dramatic. It often happens in small conversations and quiet acts of kindness. But it changes everything. It reminds me that marriage is not about perfect balance, but about showing up with grace when the other is running low.

FROM HER PERSPECTIVE

I have felt weary in seasons when responsibilities pile up faster than I can handle them. Cooking, cleaning, working, managing the emotional needs of our home, all while trying to stay steady. In those moments, what I need most is not for him to fix everything, but for him to stand with me. When he notices my tiredness and steps closer, when he offers a calm presence or quietly takes a task off my list, relief washes over me.

I have watched him grow weary too. The weight he carries is different, but the strain shows in the way he grows quiet or stares at his work longer. When I stand beside him, when I tell him I believe in him or pray with him, I see his shoulders relax. Support does not erase the challenge, but it gives us strength to face it together.

Standing together when one is weary protects our marriage from unnecessary conflict. It builds trust, creates warmth, and reminds us that we are partners in every season, not just the easy ones. It helps us keep moving when one of us needs to lean a little more.

PRAYER

Lord, teach us to recognize weariness in each other and respond with compassion. Help us stand together with patience, strength, and gentle understanding. When one of us feels overwhelmed, let the other become a steady support. Fill our home with unity so we do not face burdens alone. Give us wisdom to offer help, comfort, and encouragement. Strengthen our hearts with Your presence so that our marriage reflects Your kindness in every season. Amen.

CONVERSATION PROMPTS

1. When you are weary, what kind of support helps you most? Are there specific words, actions, or gestures that make you feel understood and safe? How can I be more present and compassionate in those moments so that you feel truly supported and not alone in what you carry?

2. What signs should I pay attention to that show you are growing tired emotionally, physically, or spiritually? How can we create rhythms in our relationship that allow rest, shared responsibility, and open conversation before weariness becomes overwhelming?

CONNECTION PRACTICES

Choose one intentional act of support for your spouse this week. It may be taking over a task they usually handle, offering a quiet moment of rest, or speaking a gentle encouragement when they seem tired. In the evening, reflect together on how this simple act lifted pressure and created closeness. End the day by thanking each other for the ways you have stood together during challenging seasons.

40. Protecting Your Marriage From Quiet Drift

Therefore we ought to give the more earnest heed to the things which we have heard, lest at any time we should let them slip.
Hebrews 2:1

Alfred Strauss was a well respected Austrian physician in early twentieth century Vienna. His wife, Marie, was known for her warmth and social involvement. In their early years, they were deeply connected, sharing long conversations in dimly lit cafés and walking through the bustling market streets hand in hand. But as Alfred's medical reputation grew, so did the demands on his time. His work consumed long hours at the hospital, and the emotional toll of caring for patients left him drained when he finally returned home.

Marie continued supporting him, hosting gatherings, managing their home, and caring for their children. Yet Alfred often sat quietly at the table, half listening, lost in the heaviness of his profession. Their conversations grew shorter. Their shared routines slowly disappeared. Neither of them intended to drift apart. It happened quietly, almost without notice.

One evening, Marie reached across the table and simply said, "I miss you." Her voice was steady, but her eyes carried both longing and sadness. Alfred looked up slowly, realizing for the first time how far the drift had carried them. He later wrote in his journals that her gentle honesty awakened him more forcefully than any argument could have.

Their marriage recovered not through sudden change, but through daily, intentional reconnection. Their drift had been silent. Their restoration became steady.

***

Drift in marriage rarely begins with conflict. Most often, it starts quietly. Responsibilities increase, routines fill, conversations shorten, and emotional attention thins. The marriage does not break. It simply loosens. Over time, distance grows in small, unspoken spaces where connection used to live.

Hebrews 2:1 offers a profound warning that fits this reality: "We must pay the most careful attention, therefore, to what we have heard, so that we do not drift away." Though written about spiritual devotion, the principle applies naturally to marriage. Drift happens not through rebellion, but through neglect. Not deliberate choice, but slow inattention.

Protecting a marriage from drift requires awareness and intentionality. It means noticing when closeness begins to fade. It means creating moments of reconnection before weariness becomes distance. It means treating emotional closeness as something to tend, not assume.

When couples give careful attention to their bond, drift loses its power. Love grows stronger, steadier, and more resilient.

***

Protecting a marriage from quiet drift requires intentional awareness. Drift does not enter loudly. It slips in through busy schedules, unspoken disappointments, and prolonged distractions. Days become crowded. Evenings become silent. Slowly, the emotional landscape shifts. The relationship begins to feel less like partnership and more like parallel living. Many couples do not realize drift has taken root until one spouse voices a longing that has gone unnoticed.

The first step in preventing drift is paying attention. Noticing changes in tone, routine, or emotional presence helps couples address distance early. Paying attention means asking questions, checking in often, and observing whether the relationship feels connected or stretched thin.

Consistency is another important safeguard. Shared rhythms anchor a marriage. Whether it is ending the day with conversation, keeping a weekly habit of connection, or pausing to pray together, these small commitments create stability. They keep the relationship from slipping beneath the weight of routine.

Emotional honesty also protects from drift. When one spouse begins feeling disconnected, speaking up early prevents resentment from building. Honest conversations require vulnerability, but vulnerability builds closeness. Silence, on the other hand, widens the space between hearts.

Time together is essential. Drift thrives in prolonged absence, whether emotional or physical. Couples who intentionally prioritize time, even in small increments, create opportunities for connection to deepen. These moments remind both spouses that their relationship remains a priority.

Protecting a marriage from drift also involves guarding against distractions. Technology, work pressure, and outside commitments can subtly steal attention. Setting healthy boundaries allows the marriage to remain centered rather than pushed to the margins.

Most importantly, preventing drift requires choosing closeness daily. It is a decision to remain present, to listen carefully, to show affection, and to nurture the bond intentionally. Over time, these choices keep the marriage strong, united, and deeply anchored.

***

FROM HIS PERSPECTIVE

I know now that drift does not arrive with warning signs. It comes quietly. It comes in the moments when I say, "I will talk to her later," or "I am too tired tonight." It comes when I begin to mistake physical proximity for real connection. There was a season when I noticed we were living beside each other rather than with each other. Nothing was wrong, yet nothing felt steady.

What shifted everything was the moment I decided to be present again. Not dramatic gestures, just small choices. Closing my laptop earlier. Sitting beside her instead of across the room. Listening fully instead of halfheartedly. Over time, these choices closed the distance I had unknowingly allowed to widen.

Drift happens easily. But reconnection happens when one spouse chooses to turn toward the other with intentionality and warmth. When she does this for me, I feel grounded again. When I do it for her, I watch her eyes soften. That softening reminds me that connection is not accidental. It is a daily act of love.

FROM HER PERSPECTIVE

There have been times when I felt the quiet ache of drift long before I could explain it. Nothing was wrong, yet something felt different. He was near but not fully present. Our conversations grew brief. Our evenings turned into parallel routines. I did not want conflict. I wanted closeness. I needed reassurance that our connection still mattered.

When he turned toward me again with intention, the drift loosened. A gentle question at the end of the day. A hand reaching for mine. A moment of eye contact that lasted long enough to communicate presence. These small choices brought comfort and warmth back into our rhythm.

I have also learned that I play a role in preventing drift. When I share my feelings honestly rather than retreating, it protects our intimacy. When I choose affection instead of silence, connection rebuilds. Drift loses its power when we both refuse to ignore distance.

Closeness is not automatic. It is protected through small, daily acts of attention. And those small acts have rebuilt our marriage many times.

PRAYER

Lord, make us alert to the quiet drift that sometimes enters our marriage. Help us notice when distance begins to form and give us courage to turn toward one another with love. Teach us to value connection, to speak gently, and to seek closeness with intention. Strengthen our bond with honesty, affection, and shared purpose. Protect our home from distraction and neglect. Keep our hearts united through every season so that our love remains steady and deeply rooted in Your grace. Amen.

CONVERSATION PROMPTS

1. Are there places where you have begun to feel even a small amount of drift between us? What moments, habits, or patterns tend to create distance for you, and how can I respond with more intention and presence so we remain emotionally close rather than slowly drifting apart?

2. What helps you feel reconnected after a period of busyness or emotional separation? Are there specific conversations, gestures, or routines that bring you back into closeness more quickly? How can we build those rhythms into our weekly life to protect our bond?

CONNECTION PRACTICES

Choose one intentional act to counter drift today. Sit together without distractions, speak one word of appreciation, or share a short moment of affection. Let this be a deliberate turning toward each other. In the evening, reflect gently on how this small act shifted the emotional tone of your day. Reinforce your closeness by ending the night with gratitude for one way your spouse chose connection.

41. Choosing Humility When Tension Rises

The sacrifices of God are a broken spirit: a broken and a contrite heart, O God, thou wilt not despise.
Psalm 51:17

The courtyard stones were still warm from the day's heat when David stepped outside to breathe. The palace around him was quiet, but his heart was anything but settled. He had spoken sharply earlier, more sharply than he intended, and the weight of it lingered heavily in the air. His frustration had been stirred by stress, not by the person he had wounded, yet the damage had been done all the same.

In the fading light, David replayed the moment. He remembered the look of surprise on the face of the servant he had spoken to, a servant who had done nothing to deserve the sting of his anger. Pride rose first, whispering that kings did not need to apologize. Yet something deeper pushed against that thought. David knew the voice of conviction when it came. He also knew what happened when he ignored it.

As he paced slowly beneath the open sky, he felt the familiar pull toward humility. He had learned the hard way that a hardened heart only multiplies pain. So he returned to the servant's quarters and spoke with sincerity. His words were simple, heartfelt, and honest.

In that small act, tension dissolved. Humility restored what pride had threatened to break. David understood again that a soft heart carries more strength than a hardened one ever could.

***

Tension rises easily in marriage. A stressful day, a misunderstood comment, or an emotional moment can spark reactions that feel larger than the situation itself. When tension builds, pride often enters quietly, urging us to defend ourselves or retreat. Yet Scripture teaches a different path.

In Psalm 51:17, David describes the sacrifice God desires: a broken spirit and a contrite heart. This posture is not weak. It is courageous. It invites healing where tension has taken root. A humble heart listens before reacting, softens before resisting, and seeks reconciliation rather than justification.

Humility also opens doors that pride closes. When spouses approach each other with gentleness after tension, walls fall. Misunderstandings shrink. Emotional safety grows stronger. Humility does not erase pain, but it clears the way for honest conversation and renewed closeness.

Choosing humility during tense moments allows couples to repair quickly, speak kindly, and remain united even when emotions rise.

***

Choosing humility when tension rises is essential for maintaining peace and emotional closeness in marriage. Tension creates moments where misunderstandings feel larger and assumptions form quickly. Without humility, tension easily turns into conflict. With humility, it becomes an opportunity for deeper understanding and connection.

Humility begins with a willingness to slow down. When emotions intensify, our instincts push us to defend, justify, or withdraw. Humility chooses to pause instead. It creates emotional space to think carefully, listen fully, and respond thoughtfully. This simple shift transforms conversations.

Another aspect of humility is acknowledging limitations. Every spouse brings their own insecurities, stresses, and blind spots into the relationship. Recognizing this truth reduces defensive reactions. It becomes easier to say, "I may not be seeing this clearly" or "I may have misunderstood." These phrases soften tension instantly.

Humility also involves taking responsibility for missteps. Even small apologies carry healing power when they come from a sincere heart. Acknowledging a sharp tone, a careless remark, or a moment of impatience repairs connection quickly. It communicates commitment to the relationship rather than commitment to being right.

Listening deeply is another expression of humility. Instead of preparing a rebuttal, humility listens to understand. It asks questions instead of assuming motives. It creates space for feelings to be expressed safely.

Humility invites empathy. When spouses choose to imagine what the other is feeling, compassion replaces irritation. Tension no longer becomes a threat but a moment to support one another.

Finally, humility aligns a marriage with God's heart. Scripture consistently shows that God draws near to the humble. When couples practice humility, they make room for His peace to steady their home. Pride dissipates. Tenderness grows. Love becomes stronger.

Humility does not remove tension, but it removes the barriers that keep tension from turning into division. In marriage, choosing humility allows two imperfect people to find unity again and again.

***

FROM HIS PERSPECTIVE

I have learned that moments of tension reveal what is happening inside me more than what is happening around me. When I respond quickly or sharply, it usually means something deeper is unsettled. Humility helps me slow down and see this truth clearly. There was a day when she asked a simple question and I reacted more strongly than the situation deserved. When I stepped away and thought about it, I realized the tension came from stress I had not acknowledged.

Choosing humility meant returning to her with honesty instead of excuses. When I apologized without defending myself, something softened between us. Her expression changed. The room felt lighter. Humility repaired what pride would have left fractured.

I am learning that humility does not diminish my strength. It protects our connection. It keeps me aware of how my words affect her. It helps me listen instead of assuming I understand everything already. When I choose humility, our relationship feels safer, calmer, and more united.

FROM HER PERSPECTIVE

Humility has changed the way I respond during tense moments. There were times when I let my emotions rise quickly and spoke before thinking. Those moments left both of us feeling misunderstood. When I began choosing humility instead of defensiveness, everything shifted. Humility helped me pause long enough to ask myself what I was truly feeling and why.

One evening, after a long day, I misunderstood something he said and reacted sharply. The room grew quiet. I felt the tension immediately, but humility reminded me not to cling to the feeling of being right. I took a breath, returned to him, and said quietly, "I think I reacted out of stress, not understanding." His face softened instantly.

Humility does not erase my voice. It strengthens it by allowing honesty without hostility. It helps me listen to him with clarity instead of assumption. It helps me admit when I have misunderstood. Most of all, it keeps our hearts connected even when the situation is difficult.

Humility makes room for peace where tension once tried to settle.

PRAYER

Lord, help us choose humility when tension rises. Teach us to pause before reacting and to listen with compassion instead of defensiveness. Soften our hearts so we can approach each other with gentleness and honesty. Give us wisdom to speak truth in love and courage to apologize when needed. Let humility shape our conversations, protect our connection, and strengthen the unity in our marriage. Fill our home with peace that comes from following Your ways. Amen.

CONVERSATION PROMPTS

1. When tension rises between us, what helps you feel safe and understood instead of pressured or misunderstood? Are there specific words, tones, or approaches that make it easier for you to stay open rather than shutting down? How can I practice humility in those moments so our connection remains steady?

2. What makes it difficult for you to choose humility during tense conversations? Are there past experiences, fears, or patterns that influence how you respond under pressure? How can we gently support each other so humility becomes our natural response, not our last resort?

CONNECTION PRACTICES

This week, choose one moment during a tense or stressful situation to intentionally practice humility. Pause before reacting, offer a soft response, or ask a clarifying question. At the end of the day, reflect together on how humility changed the tone of the moment and whether it helped you feel closer rather than distant. Close your conversation with one word of appreciation for the humility you saw in each other.

42. Learning to Communicate with Patience

A soft answer turneth away wrath: but grievous words stir up anger.
Proverbs 15:1

Franklin and Eleanor Roosevelt's marriage was shaped by both remarkable strength and profound difficulty. Their public lives demanded constant attention, yet it was the quieter, private moments that tested them most. During Franklin's early political years, his schedule became increasingly demanding. Meetings, travel, and public duties consumed his days. Eleanor, who carried heavy responsibilities of her own, sometimes felt distant from him, unsure how to reach past the noise surrounding their life.

There was a period when tension grew quietly between them. Conversations became rushed, filled more with logistics than connection. Misunderstandings appeared easily. Franklin, exhausted from political pressure, sometimes spoke too quickly. Eleanor's strong sense of purpose occasionally pushed her into abruptness. They were devoted, yet their communication faltered under the weight of unspoken frustrations.

One evening, after a particularly strained conversation, Eleanor wrote a letter to Franklin instead of speaking face to face. Her tone was gentle, honest, and patient. She expressed her concerns without accusation. Franklin later described the letter as a turning point. Her patience softened his defenses, helping him hear what she could not have said easily aloud.

Their communication improved slowly through thoughtful effort. Her patience helped steady his responses. His willingness to listen rebuilt trust.

Their story shows how patient communication can heal tensions that hurried words only deepen.

***

Communication in marriage often shapes the atmosphere of the home more than circumstances do. Stress, fatigue, and misunderstandings can make responses sharper and conversations shorter. When couples speak quickly, frustration grows. When they slow down and use gentle words, connection becomes easier to restore.

Proverbs 15:1 gives a simple yet transformative truth: "A gentle answer turns away wrath, but a harsh word stirs up anger." This wisdom applies directly to marriage. Patience in communication is not silence. It is choosing calmness over reaction. It is responding with understanding instead of defensiveness.

Patience creates space for clarity. It helps both spouses express themselves without fear of escalation. It invites thoughtful listening rather than rushed assumptions. When couples choose patient communication, conflicts shrink instead of spreading.

Patience does not ignore wrongdoing or minimize feelings. It simply protects the conversation from becoming harmful. It allows both hearts to remain open long enough to find real understanding.

***

Learning to communicate with patience strengthens every part of a marriage. Patience creates an emotional environment where words can be heard, understood, and respected. Without patience, conversations become brief, tense, or easily misinterpreted. With patience, even difficult topics can be explored safely.

Patience begins with awareness. When tension rises, it becomes easy to speak quickly or interrupt. Patience invites spouses to pause before responding. This simple pause reduces misunderstandings and prevents small irritations from becoming large conflicts.

Listening is a major part of patient communication. Listening patiently means focusing on understanding rather than preparing a response. It means giving full attention instead of dividing it with distractions. When spouses listen patiently, they communicate value and respect. They show the other person that their feelings matter deeply.

Patience also includes tone. The same words can heal or harm depending on how they are spoken. A gentle tone communicates openness, while a sharp tone creates distance. When spouses are mindful of tone, conversations stay soft even when the topic is difficult.

Patience helps couples speak honestly without fear. In patient communication, vulnerability feels safe. A spouse can share disappointment, confusion, or worry without expecting anger in return. This builds emotional intimacy and trust.

Another benefit is emotional control. Patience allows spouses to slow their reactions. It gives space for emotions to settle before words are spoken. This prevents regret and strengthens unity.

Finally, patient communication reflects God's heart. Scripture shows Him slow to anger and rich in love. When couples practice patience, they reflect this divine gentleness in their home.

Patience does not mean avoiding truth. It means speaking truth with kindness. It means approaching tension with understanding instead of force. Over time, patient communication builds a marriage filled with peace, clarity, and deep connection.

***

FROM HIS PERSPECTIVE

I have learned that the way I speak affects her more deeply than I sometimes realize. When I rush my words or respond from stress, I see the hurt in her eyes even if she tries to hide it. Patience in communication is not easy for me, especially when I feel pressured or distracted. But the more I practice slowing down, the more I notice how it changes the tone of our entire home.

There was a moment recently when she shared something heavy, and my first instinct was to offer a solution. Instead, I chose patience. I listened without jumping ahead. She relaxed. Her shoulders softened. She opened up even more. I realized in that moment that patient listening is often more powerful than any advice I could offer.

When she communicates patiently with me, I feel safe admitting my weaknesses. I feel understood, not judged. Her patience gives me space to process my thoughts without pressure.

Patient communication does not remove conflict. It simply keeps conflict from becoming damaging. It teaches me to love her with gentleness in my words and steadiness in my tone.

FROM HER PERSPECTIVE

Patient communication changes the way we handle stress. When I speak quickly, especially out of frustration, he closes off. When I slow down and choose gentleness, he feels safe enough to share what is going on inside him. Patience turns difficult conversations into opportunities for closeness instead of conflict.

There was an evening when I felt overwhelmed and misunderstood. My emotions were high, and I was tempted to react sharply. But I took a breath and spoke calmly instead. The entire direction of our conversation shifted. He listened carefully, and I felt comfort instead of distance.

When he practices patient communication with me, I feel cherished. His tone, his willingness to pause, and his desire to understand tell me that I matter to him. It is in these moments that I see his love most clearly.

Patience in communication creates emotional safety. It reminds me that we are a team. It teaches me to speak with kindness and to listen with intention. When we both choose patience, our marriage stays grounded even in stressful seasons.

PRAYER

Lord, teach us to communicate with patience and gentleness. Help us slow our reactions, soften our tone, and listen with genuine understanding. Guard our hearts from quick anger and strengthen our desire to respond with kindness. Fill our conversations with clarity, compassion, and wisdom so that we draw closer, not apart. Let our communication reflect Your peace and Your love. Guide our words, calm our emotions, and shape our home with patience that honors You. Amen.

CONVERSATION PROMPTS

1. When tension rises in our conversations, what helps you feel heard and understood rather than rushed or dismissed? Are there specific tones, phrases, or approaches that bring you comfort when discussing difficult topics? I want to learn how to communicate with more patience so you feel emotionally safe and valued.

2. What habits do you think we could adjust to make our communication more patient and peaceful? Are there patterns of distraction, frustration, or timing that hinder deeper connection? How can we work together to create conversations that stay calm, open, and gentle even when the subject is heavy?

CONNECTION PRACTICES

Choose one moment today to practice patient communication. Slow your tone, listen without interrupting, or pause before responding. Be intentional in your presence. At the end of the day, reflect together on how this gentle pacing shaped the conversation and whether it brought more peace into your connection. End your time by affirming one patient choice you noticed in each other.

43. Offering Reassurance in Times of Doubt

Fear thou not; for I am with thee: be not dismayed;
for I am thy God: I will strengthen thee; yea, I will help thee;
yea, I will uphold thee with the right hand of my righteousness.
Isaiah 41:10

The wind moved quietly across the desert stones as Elijah walked alone beneath the fading sky. Only a day earlier, he had stood on Mount Carmel, calling on the Lord with bold confidence. Fire had fallen. The people had seen God's power. Strength surged through him then. But now, in the stillness, fear and exhaustion pressed against his heart with surprising force.

Elijah sat beneath a broom tree, resting his head in his hands. Doubt crept in silently. He wondered if he had accomplished anything at all. He wondered if his life's work mattered. He wondered if he could continue. His confidence, so strong the day before, felt thin now. Despair settled where courage once stood.

In his weariness, Elijah whispered, "It is enough." His heart felt fragile, and his future felt uncertain. Yet God did not rebuke him. Instead, an angel touched him gently and said, "Get up and eat." Later, God met Elijah not in wind or fire, but in a gentle whisper that reassured his trembling heart.

Elijah's story shows how even the strongest can face doubt. And it reveals a deeper truth: reassurance offered in gentle, steady ways can restore a weary soul more powerfully than strength alone.

***

Doubt touches every marriage at various points. Even strong spouses face moments when they question their value, their choices, or their abilities. These doubts may appear quietly, through hesitation in their voice or heaviness in their posture. When one spouse feels unsure, the reassurance of the other becomes a lifeline.

Isaiah 41:10 offers a powerful truth that fits these moments: "Do not fear, for I am with you. Do not be dismayed, for I am your God." God reassures with presence, not pressure. He speaks comfort before correction, calm before direction. His reassurance strengthens confidence without dismissing emotion.

In marriage, offering reassurance follows this same pattern. It means listening without minimizing fears. It means speaking truth gently, reminding your spouse of their worth, their strength, and the good you see in them. Reassurance does not rush. It restores.

Moments of doubt do not signal weakness in the marriage. They create opportunities for deeper closeness, tenderness, and trust.

***

Offering reassurance in times of doubt strengthens the emotional foundation of a marriage. Doubt arrives quietly, often when stress, fatigue, or disappointment seep into the heart. It can make a spouse question their abilities, their value, or whether they are doing enough. In these moments, reassurance becomes an essential expression of love.

Reassurance begins with presence. When one spouse feels uncertain, the other's steady presence communicates safety. Sitting close, listening fully, and giving time for vulnerability help remove the fear of being misunderstood. Presence speaks reassurance before any words are spoken.

Another part of reassurance is affirming truth. Doubt often magnifies weakness and hides strength. Gentle reminders of character, effort, and growth help reshape perspective. When spouses speak truth in kindness, hope rises again. Words such as "I believe in you" or "You are not alone" carry enormous emotional weight.

Reassurance requires patience. Doubt does not disappear quickly. A spouse may need repeated comfort before confidence returns. Patience allows space for processing, reflection, and healing. When reassurance is offered consistently, trust deepens.

Practical support also reassures. Helping with burdens, sharing responsibilities, or stepping into a stressful situation communicates, "We will face this together." These actions reinforce emotional security.

Emotional attentiveness is equally important. When one spouse notices small signs of discouragement, their gentle check ins can prevent doubt from growing. Asking thoughtful questions and offering comfort before the doubt becomes heavy shows deep care.

Reassurance also reflects God's character. Scripture repeatedly shows Him strengthening the weary and speaking peace to troubled hearts. Couples who offer reassurance imitate this divine gentleness, bringing spiritual strength into their marriage.

Finally, reassurance builds resilience. When spouses learn to support each other in doubt, they create a marriage capable of withstanding uncertainty and change. Their bond becomes rooted not only in joy, but in steady, compassionate support.

Reassurance may seem small in the moment, but it builds a marriage where both hearts feel safe, valued, and deeply connected.

FROM HIS PERSPECTIVE

There are moments when doubt settles into my thoughts quietly. It may come after a difficult day, a mistake at work, or a feeling that I am not doing enough for our family. In those moments, I tend to withdraw. I do not always show it, but the weight sits heavy inside. When she notices and offers reassurance, something inside me steadies. Her words remind me of who I am, not just how I feel. She speaks to the strength she sees, even when I cannot see it myself.

I am learning that reassurance is not about fixing everything. It is about being present with a tender heart. When she faces doubt, I have seen how much it means when I speak gently, listen fully, and remind her that she is valued. Reassurance changes the atmosphere. It pulls us closer, removes fear, and makes vulnerability safe.

When doubt enters, reassurance becomes a gift that strengthens us both.

FROM HER PERSPECTIVE

There are days when doubt comes in subtle waves. I question my decisions, my abilities, or whether I am doing enough for our home and children. During those times, a single gentle reassurance from him can feel like sunlight breaking through clouds. When he tells me I am doing well, or when he notices the effort I put in, it settles something deep inside my heart. His reassurance does not erase the challenge, but it reminds me that I am not walking through it alone.

I am also learning to reassure him when I see doubt in his eyes. When I remind him of his strength, his integrity, and the way our family depends on him, I watch encouragement return to his posture. Reassurance is not dramatic. It is spoken with quiet conviction, steady presence, and genuine love.

In moments of doubt, reassurance becomes the bridge that brings us together again.

PRAYER

Lord, teach us to offer reassurance when doubt enters our marriage. Help us listen with compassion, speak with gentleness, and recognize the deeper needs beneath each other's fears. Strengthen our hearts so we can remind one another of truth, worth, and Your constant presence. Guide our words so they bring comfort rather than pressure. Fill our home with hope and steady grace. As we reassure each other, draw us closer to You and to one another. Amen.

CONVERSATION PROMPTS

1. When you feel doubt rising in your heart, what type of reassurance helps you most? Are there specific words, gestures, or tones that make you feel supported and safe? I want to understand how to respond with tenderness so that doubt does not isolate you but instead brings us closer.

2. Are there areas in your life where you struggle with doubt more often, such as work, parenting, faith, or personal identity? How can I speak into these places with encouragement and steady support, offering comfort without pressure and reassurance without minimizing your feelings?

CONNECTION PRACTICES

Today, offer one intentional reassurance to your spouse in an area where you know they often feel uncertain. Speak gently, affirm something true about their character or effort, and give them space to receive it. At the end of the day, share how that reassurance shaped your connection and whether it brought comfort or clarity. Close your evening by expressing gratitude for one way your spouse strengthened you this week.

44. Finding Strength in Shared Worship

O magnify the Lord with me, and let us exalt his name together.
Psalm 34:3

The smoke rose in thin, twisting columns above the horizon long before David and his men reached Ziklag. The closer they rode, the more dread tightened in their chests. When they finally arrived, the camp lay in ruins. Homes burned. Supplies scattered. And worst of all, the women and children were gone. The Amalekites had swept through like a storm, leaving nothing but ashes behind.

Grief broke the men open. They wept until their strength was gone. Anger followed quickly. Whispers turned into accusations, and soon all eyes turned toward David. The weight of despair pressed so heavily that the men considered turning against him entirely.

David stood in the midst of devastation, his own heart shattered. His family was gone too. Yet in the swirl of fear, blame, and heartbreak, David did something quietly powerful. He stepped aside and sought the Lord. Scripture says he "strengthened himself in the Lord his God."

When he returned, something in him had shifted. His voice held steadiness where panic had been. His presence brought calm where fear had spread. His worship grounded him, and that grounding strengthened everyone around him.

The turning point came not from strategy or commands, but from shared faith that steadied weary hearts in the face of loss.

***

Shared worship strengthens marriage in ways nothing else can. When two hearts turn together toward God, fear loses its grip, tension loosens, and unity grows deeper. Worship is not limited to singing. It is the posture of seeking God together, trusting Him together, and inviting His peace into the center of the home.

Psalm 34:3 captures this beautifully. "Oh, magnify the Lord with me, and let us exalt His name together." Worship unites. It shifts focus from fear to faith, from self to God, from uncertainty to His steady presence.

In marriage, shared worship reminds spouses that they are not fighting battles alone. It anchors decisions, calms anxieties, and brings clarity when emotions cloud perspective. When couples pray, read Scripture, or seek the Lord side by side, their hearts align in a way that strengthens their relationship deeply.

Shared worship does not ignore hardship. It brings God's strength into the middle of it.

***

Finding strength in shared worship creates a foundation of unity that carries a marriage through every season. Worship pulls both hearts toward the same source of peace, wisdom, and direction. It becomes the steady center that holds a couple together when life feels overwhelming.

Shared worship builds connection. When couples turn to God together, they share vulnerability, honesty, and spiritual hope. It softens tension because it reminds both hearts that God is bigger than any moment of stress. It quiets pride because worship draws attention away from winning and toward surrender. It strengthens intimacy because seeking God together brings emotional closeness that cannot be manufactured in any other way.

Shared worship also brings clarity. When spouses worship, whether through prayer, Scripture, or quiet reflection, God often brings insight that guides decisions and restores peace. Instead of relying solely on their own strength or perspective, couples learn to rely on God's leading.

Worship cultivates gratitude. In the middle of difficulty, shared worship helps couples remember what God has done before. Gratitude shifts the emotional atmosphere of the home, lifting discouragement and strengthening hope.

Shared worship also provides stability. When one spouse is discouraged, the other can help lift their gaze upward. When both are weary, God becomes their shared refuge. Worship gently reminds them that their story is held by Someone who sees beyond the present moment.

Another key benefit is that worship reduces isolation. Difficult seasons can make couples feel alone even while sharing the same home. When they worship together, isolation breaks. The act of seeking God side by side becomes a tether that keeps their hearts connected.

Finally, shared worship invites God's presence into the marriage. His peace, His strength, and His wisdom fill the spaces where fear once sat.

Shared worship does not require perfection. It requires willingness. A willing heart creates a marriage grounded in God's steady grace.

FROM HIS PERSPECTIVE

There are nights when my thoughts feel tangled and my confidence thin. When Emeline sits beside me and we pray or read Scripture together, my heart steadies. I feel our unity strengthen. I feel God's presence moving the tension out of the room. Shared worship reminds me that I do not carry our burdens alone. When she lifts her voice or speaks a simple prayer, it reaches places in me that my own strength cannot.

I also see what worship does for us as a couple. It softens me. It helps me listen more carefully, respond more gently, and lead with humility. When we worship, I feel my priorities realigning. The things that seemed overwhelming become smaller. The love I have for her feels deeper, stronger, and more rooted in something eternal.

Shared worship is not dramatic. It is simple. But it changes everything.

FROM HER PERSPECTIVE

When we worship together, my heart feels grounded. There are days when emotions rise quickly or when worry settles in my chest, and worship brings the calm I cannot find elsewhere. Hearing Emmett pray, watching him turn to God, or sitting beside him with Scripture open reminds me that our strength does not come from perfection. It comes from God's presence in our home.

Shared worship makes me feel safe. It reassures me that we are walking in the same direction. It lifts my spirit and reminds me that the burdens we carry are held by

Someone stronger than both of us. When we worship together, misunderstandings soften, tension loosens, and our home feels filled with peace again.

Worship connects us in a deep and gentle way. It keeps our hearts close even when life feels chaotic.

PRAYER

Lord, teach us to seek You together. Fill our home with the peace that comes from shared worship. Strengthen us when we grow weary and unite our hearts as we turn toward You. Help us find comfort, clarity, and renewed love in Your presence. Guide our conversations, calm our worries, and remind us that we are held securely by Your grace. Let shared worship deepen our connection and create a refuge of faith within our marriage. Amen.

CONVERSATION PROMPTS

1. What forms of worship help you feel closest to God, and how can I join you in those moments? Are there ways we can create simple rhythms of shared worship that help us grow spiritually while staying emotionally connected, even during busy weeks or stressful seasons?

2. When we face difficult days, what kind of spiritual support from me helps you feel strengthened rather than pressured? How can we encourage each other to seek God together in a rhythm that feels natural, peaceful, and meaningful for both of us?

CONNECTION PRACTICES

Choose one simple act of shared worship this week: pray together briefly, read one verse aloud, or spend a moment thanking God together. Keep it gentle and unhurried. At the end of the day, reflect on how that small spiritual connection shaped your emotions and your closeness. Express one gratitude for how your spouse helps you grow spiritually.

45. Staying Present in a Busy Season

So teach us to number our days, that
we may apply our hearts unto wisdom.
Psalm 90:12

It was one of those stretches of life when everything seemed to happen at once. Work deadlines arrived back to back. The kids had projects, practices, and appointments packed into the same week. Even weekends filled quickly with errands that kept piling up. One evening, after the house finally grew quiet, Emeline sat on the couch feeling both drained and strangely distant from Emmet, even though he was only a few feet away working through emails.

Their friend Lydia had come by earlier to return a book. When she stepped inside, she paused and said gently, "You both look like you have run five marathons in a row." She laughed softly, but there was understanding in her eyes. She and her husband had gone through a similar season the year before, and she knew how easy it was for busyness to quietly steal connection.

Before Lydia left, she said something that stayed with them. "You cannot wait for life to slow down before being present with each other. Busy seasons tend to multiply, not shrink. Presence is something you choose even when the pace feels relentless."

Later that night, Emmet closed his laptop and sat beside Emeline. They did not say much at first. They simply leaned against each other, choosing presence over pressure.

It was small, but it was enough to draw their hearts close again.

***

Busy seasons do not always arrive with warning. They sweep in suddenly, filling days with tasks and minds with lists. In these moments, emotional presence can slip without notice. Communication becomes brief. Affection gets delayed. Togetherness becomes something postponed rather than practiced. This quiet drift is one of the most common sources of disconnection in marriage.

Psalm 90:12 offers a gentle reminder: "Teach us to number our days, that we may gain a heart of wisdom." Wisdom teaches us that time is fragile. Days pass quickly, and relationships require intentional presence even when schedules feel overwhelming.

Staying present in busy seasons does not require hours of uninterrupted time. It requires attention. It requires choosing to pause, look at one another, listen fully, and share small moments of connection.

Presence communicates love without needing perfection. It keeps the heart steady even when the pace of life becomes demanding.

***

Staying present in a busy season is one of the most powerful gifts a couple can give each other. Busyness is not the enemy, but unexamined busyness often becomes one. When days fill with tasks, appointments, and responsibilities, presence becomes harder to maintain. Couples may move through the same rooms without truly seeing each other. Yet presence is what keeps the marriage emotionally alive during hectic times.

Presence begins with awareness. When tensions rise or schedules intensify, couples can choose to notice small signs of disconnection. A shorter tone, fewer shared moments, or increasing silence are invitations to pause. Presence means stopping long enough to ask, “How are you truly doing today”

It also involves intentionality. Presence does not happen automatically. It grows through small, deliberate choices: sitting together for a few minutes, offering a warm touch in passing, or ending the day with a moment of quiet conversation. These small investments nourish emotional closeness.

Listening is another essential aspect. In busy seasons, listening can become rushed or shallow. Staying present means listening with full attention, even for brief moments. It communicates value and protects the relationship from thinning.

Presence also requires boundaries. Not every task deserves priority over connection. Couples who protect small spaces of time remain emotionally anchored. Even a brief moment of slowing down together can reset the tone of an entire week.

Shared rest is important as well. Busy seasons drain energy, making it easy to withdraw. Taking small pauses together, even simple ones like stepping outside for a breath of fresh air or sharing a quiet meal, reinforces unity.

Finally, staying present in busy seasons reflects wisdom. It demonstrates awareness that days pass quickly and that marriage must be nurtured intentionally. When couples choose presence, they safeguard their bond from quiet drift and strengthen their connection in every season.

***

FROM HIS PERSPECTIVE

When life becomes busy, my mind begins to fill with tasks, deadlines, and responsibilities. I do not always notice how quickly I drift into distraction. There are moments when Emeline talks and I hear the words but not the heart behind them. I remember one evening when she touched my arm and said softly, “I miss you, even though you are right here.” It stopped me. I realized I had been physically present but mentally and emotionally elsewhere.

Staying present takes effort, especially when I feel stretched thin. But I have seen how much it matters. When I choose to stop, look at her, and listen fully, I feel something soften inside me. I feel our connection return. Presence brings calm that busyness cannot offer. It anchors both of us.

I am learning that presence is not about long conversations or grand gestures. It is about attention. It is about choosing her in the middle of stress rather than after the stress passes. When I stay present with her, even for a few minutes, our home feels steadier and our relationship feels alive again.

FROM HER PERSPECTIVE

Busy seasons affect me differently. I start moving faster, thinking ahead constantly, and trying to hold everything together. In the middle of it, I sometimes forget to slow down long enough to connect with him. I forget that my presence matters as much as my productivity. When Emmett reaches for my hand or asks how I am doing with genuine attention, it brings relief. It reminds me I am not carrying everything alone.

I also notice when he begins to drift into his own busyness. Instead of assuming he is uninterested, I am learning to gently invite him back into connection. A simple question or a moment of quiet closeness can ease the pressure on both of us.

Presence in busy seasons keeps our hearts aligned. It reminds me that we are partners, not two people moving in separate lanes. When we choose to be present, even briefly, I feel grounded. I feel loved. I feel safe. Presence does not erase the busyness, but it protects our relationship from being swallowed by it.

PRAYER

Lord, teach us to stay present with each other even when life becomes full. Help us slow our pace, notice one another, and give attention with sincerity. Protect our hearts from drifting during busy seasons. Strengthen our connection through small, meaningful moments of closeness. Fill our home with Your peace so we do not lose sight of what matters most. Guide us to create space for each other with tenderness, patience, and intentional love. Amen.

CONVERSATION PROMPTS

1. During busy seasons, what helps you feel emotionally connected to me instead of overlooked or rushed? Are there specific moments, gestures, or rhythms that strengthen your sense of closeness even when our schedules are full? I want to understand how to make presence a priority in the ways that matter most to you.

2. When life feels fast, what causes you to disconnect or feel distant more quickly? Are there stress patterns, distractions, or habits that make you feel less seen? How can we create ways to gently pull each other back into connection before the distance grows?

CONNECTION PRACTICES

Choose one small moment today to practice presence. Put aside distractions, pause your routine, and look at each other with full attention. Share a brief conversation or a quiet moment of closeness. Later, reflect on whether that simple act softened the pace of the day or restored calm. End with one sentence of gratitude for the presence your spouse offered.

46. Supporting Each Other Through Unexpected Change

Be careful for nothing; but in every thing by prayer and supplication
with thanksgiving let your requests be made known unto God.
And the peace of God, which passeth all understanding,
shall keep your hearts and minds through Christ Jesus.
Philippians 4:6–7

In the early years of the twentieth century, explorer Ernest Shackleton prepared for one of the most dangerous expeditions ever attempted. While his voyages became legendary, far fewer people know the steady presence behind the scenes. His wife, Emily Shackleton, quietly carried burdens that never reached headlines. When Ernest set out on the Endurance expedition, Emily stepped into a season filled with uncertainty, financial strain, and long stretches without news. Letters from him arrived only occasionally, often months late.

During those years, their world changed rapidly. Ernest faced brutal ice storms and shipwreck. Emily faced the emotional weight of not knowing if her husband was even alive. Yet in the absence of certainty, she chose steadiness. Her letters were filled not with panic, but with calm encouragement. She reassured him of her support, anchored their household, and protected their children emotionally. Her strength became a lifeline to Ernest, whose own words reveal how deeply he relied on her resilience.

When he finally returned, weary but alive, he often credited her for sustaining him through the darkest months. Their story shows that unexpected change does not have to fracture a marriage. With support, steadiness, and shared hope, it can strengthen it instead.

***

Unexpected change brings pressure to a marriage. Even strong relationships feel the strain when life shifts suddenly. New responsibilities appear. Plans collapse. Emotions intensify. In these moments, panic can rise quickly. Support becomes essential.

Philippians 4:6–7 offers a calming truth that steadies the heart in seasons like these. "Do not be anxious about anything, but in everything, by prayer and supplication with thanksgiving, present your requests to God. And the peace of God, which surpasses all understanding, will guard your hearts and your minds in Christ Jesus." This peace is not passive. It is protective. It guards the heart when fear tries to enter.

Supporting each other through unexpected change reflects this same truth. It means offering calm when the situation feels unstable. It means turning toward each other rather than away. It means choosing prayer instead of panic and encouragement instead of criticism.

When couples face change together, God's peace strengthens them beyond what circumstances can shake.

***

Supporting each other through unexpected change is one of the most vital roles within marriage. Life often shifts without warning. Illness, job transitions, financial strain, new responsibilities, and emotional challenges arrive suddenly. These moments can create stress, confusion, and fear. Yet they can also become opportunities for unity, tenderness, and growth.

Support begins with presence. When change hits, the first need is often simple: to know you are not alone. A calm voice, a soft touch, or a quiet moment together steadies the heart. Presence strengthens courage.

Another part of support is emotional attentiveness. Couples who notice each other's fears, hesitations, and unspoken worries respond with compassion rather than pressure. This attentiveness reduces fear and builds trust.

Support also includes shared responsibility. Unexpected change often increases the load one spouse must carry. Helping practically, adjusting routines, or stepping into temporary burdens communicates deep love. It says, "We will face this together."

Communication plays an important role. Change can bring misunderstandings or hidden assumptions. Honest, gentle conversations prevent frustration and keep both spouses moving in the same direction. Supportive communication reassures, clarifies, and restores peace.

Prayer strengthens everything. When couples bring unexpected change before God, fear loses its grip. Prayer reminds them that God sees what they cannot, carries what they cannot, and steadies what feels fragile. His peace fills the gaps where human strength runs thin.

Finally, support during unexpected change deepens resilience. Couples who walk through upheaval together emerge with a stronger bond. Their trust grows. Their appreciation for each other increases. Their unity becomes rooted not only in joy, but in shared courage and faith.

Supporting one another through unexpected change does not remove hardship. It transforms it into a path of deeper connection.

FROM HIS PERSPECTIVE

Unexpected change always reveals something inside me. Sometimes it is confidence. Sometimes it is fear. There have been moments when life shifted suddenly and left me unsure of what to do next. During those times, my wife's calm presence became my anchor. Even before we solved anything, her steadiness reassured me that we could face the uncertainty together. I remember one evening when news arrived that changed our plans completely. She sat beside me silently, her hand on mine. That silence carried more comfort than any solution could have offered.

As I learn to support her through unexpected change, I see how much peace it brings. When I slow down, listen to her fears without interrupting, and reassure her that we will navigate this together, something softens in her. Her breathing steadies. Her shoulders relax. I realize support is not about fixing everything. It is about being present, patient, and calm. It is walking through the unknown side by side.

FROM HER PERSPECTIVE

Change affects me deeply. When something unexpected happens, my mind immediately begins spinning through possibilities, responsibilities, and what needs to be done next. This can make me feel overwhelmed quickly. When Emmett steps in with calm reassurance, it changes everything. His presence helps me slow down. His steady voice helps me breathe again. There was a moment not long ago when sudden news turned my plans upside down. He simply said, "We will do this together." Those few words dissolved the pressure inside me.

Supporting him through unexpected change has taught me patience. He processes differently. He needs time to think. He needs space to quietly gather courage. When I sit beside him, speak gently, and listen without rushing him, I watch his confidence return. Change may shake our circumstances, but support steadies our connection. We learn to lean into each other rather than letting fear push us apart.

PRAYER

Lord, help us support each other with gentleness when unexpected change enters our lives. Calm our fears and steady our hearts. Teach us to listen with compassion and speak with reassurance. Guide us to stand together rather than reacting in isolation. Fill our home with Your peace, the peace that guards our minds and hearts when circumstances shift. Help us trust that You are present in every transition and faithful in every season. Unite us through every uncertainty. Amen.

CONVERSATION PROMPTS

1. When unexpected change happens, what tends to worry you most? Are there specific ways I can support you that help you feel calmer and more grounded? I want to understand the kind of presence and encouragement that reassures you most when life shifts suddenly.

2. When you think about unexpected changes from the past, what responses from me brought comfort and what responses made things harder? How can we communicate better and support one another more intentionally when new challenges appear without warning?

CONNECTION PRACTICES

Choose one area of uncertainty, even a small one, and face it intentionally together this week. Share your thoughts, pray briefly, and offer reassurance to each other. Take a few minutes in the evening to reflect on how this shared approach brought comfort or unity. End the night by naming one new thing you appreciate about your spouse's strength during change.

47. Handling Disappointment with Grace

Why art thou cast down, O my soul?
why art thou disquieted in me? hope thou in God:
for I shall yet praise him for the help of his countenance.
Psalm 42:5

It happened on a Tuesday evening, the kind of evening neither of them expected to become memorable. Emmet had been preparing for weeks to present a project that he believed might open a new door for his team at work. He returned home later than usual, quiet, with a stiffness in his shoulders that told Emeline something had gone wrong before he even spoke. She paused her dinner prep, wiped her hands on a towel, and looked at him.

"They rejected it," he said finally. His voice was calm, but his eyes carried the weight of disappointment. He had hoped for more. He had poured himself into the work. Now the opportunity had slipped away.

Emeline walked over, rested her hand lightly on his chest, and whispered, "I am sorry. I know how much this meant to you." They stood together for a quiet moment, the hum of the refrigerator filling the space between them.

Later that night, after the kids were in bed, they sat on the couch with the lights dimmed. Emmet talked through everything he wished had gone differently. Emeline listened, not offering solutions, only presence. What surprised both of them was how much comfort came not from fixing the disappointment, but from holding it together.

***

Disappointment can unsettle the heart more deeply than many other emotions. It makes hope feel thin and outcomes feel unfair. In marriage, disappointment does not belong to only one person. It affects the atmosphere of the home, the tone of conversations, and the way a spouse carries themselves. Grace becomes essential in moments like these.

Psalm 42:5 asks, "Why are you cast down, O my soul, and why are you in turmoil within me Put your hope in God." This verse acknowledges the weight of disappointment honestly. It does not silence the feeling. It guides the heart toward hope.

When a spouse faces disappointment, offering grace means listening without judgment, giving space without distance, and speaking encouragement without pressure. Grace does not rush healing. It simply stands near with a calm and steady presence.

Marriage becomes stronger when spouses learn to support each other through the gentle, quiet work of carrying disappointment together.

***

Handling disappointment with grace is an essential part of building emotional closeness in marriage. Disappointment touches everyone eventually. It may arise from work situations, personal goals, relationships, parenting challenges, or unmet expectations. When disappointment enters a marriage, it can either isolate or unite the couple. Grace determines which direction it moves.

Grace begins with empathy. When one spouse feels the sting of unmet expectation, the other can offer a listening ear without trying to fix the situation immediately. Empathy acknowledges pain without dismissing it. It communicates, "I am with you," even when words feel inadequate.

Another part of grace is patience. Disappointment rarely resolves quickly. Some disappointments fade within days, while others linger longer. Patience allows space for processing. It prevents frustration from adding pressure to an already heavy heart. When spouses give each other room to feel, healing becomes steadier and more complete.

Grace also means guarding tone and timing. Disappointment can make emotions fragile. Gentle words protect the relationship during vulnerable moments. Overly quick advice or criticism can deepen discouragement. Grace speaks slowly and softly.

Practical support strengthens the expression of grace. Simple acts such as making space for rest, taking over a task, or creating a comforting environment communicate love more loudly than speeches. These gestures remind the discouraged spouse that they do not walk alone.

Prayer also plays a vital role. Bringing disappointment before God aligns hearts with His peace and His perspective. Couples who pray together during discouraging moments find courage that rises quietly, grounding them in hope.

Finally, grace turns disappointment into connection rather than tension. A marriage shaped by grace does not collapse under unmet expectations. It grows stronger as both spouses learn to hold each other's hearts gently. Handling disappointment with grace becomes a shared practice that deepens emotional safety, trust, and unity.

***

FROM HIS PERSPECTIVE

When disappointment hits me, I tend to withdraw at first. I replay the situation in my mind, picking apart details and wondering what I should have done differently. There are moments when I do not want to talk right away, not because I want distance, but because I need a moment to breathe. What helps most is when Emeline gives me space without stepping away emotionally. When she sits beside me quietly or listens without pressure, I feel something inside begin to ease.

One thing I have realized is how much her gentle presence matters. She does not try to erase the disappointment or pretend it is small. She simply offers grace, and that grace lifts the heaviness more than anything else. When I am ready to talk and she responds with understanding instead of quick solutions, I feel supported. Disappointment still hurts, but it does not feel lonely.

FROM HER PERSPECTIVE

Disappointment affects me deeply, sometimes more than I expect. When something I hoped for does not work out, I feel the letdown in both my mind and my heart. I can become quiet, thoughtful, and unsure of what I need. What comforts me most is when he notices without pushing. When Emmett says, "I am here if you want to talk," or simply holds my hand, I feel understood.

There was a time when something I had been working toward fell through suddenly. I felt embarrassed and discouraged. He sat beside me and said, "This does not define you." Those simple words lifted a weight I had been carrying silently. His grace helped me regain confidence.

When he offers patience and gentleness during disappointment, I feel safe enough to share honestly. His grace gives me room to process without fear of judgment. It strengthens our bond in ways that joy alone cannot.

PRAYER

Lord, teach us to offer grace when disappointment enters our marriage. Help us listen with compassion, speak with tenderness, and support each other without pressure. Calm the thoughts that spiral and steady our hearts with Your peace. Remind us that disappointment is not the end of our story and that You remain faithful in every season. Guide us to walk through discouraging moments with unity, patience, and love. Amen.

CONVERSATION PROMPTS

1. When you feel disappointed, what kind of support helps you feel understood and safe rather than overwhelmed or alone? Are there specific gestures, words, or rhythms that bring you comfort during discouraging moments?

2. What kinds of disappointments tend to affect you most deeply, and how can we navigate those moments as a team? Are there ways I can be more present or attentive when your heart feels heavy?

CONNECTION PRACTICES

Choose one moment this week to offer unexpected encouragement to your spouse in an area where you know they have felt disappointment. Speak gently, affirm their value, and offer small support without being asked. At the end of the day, reflect together on whether this lifted their heart or strengthened your connection. End by sharing one hope you are praying for together.

48. Choosing Kindness When Frustration Rises

And be ye kind one to another, tenderhearted, forgiving one another, even as God for Christ's sake hath forgiven you.
Ephesians 4:32

Charles Spurgeon was known across England for his preaching, but the quieter story behind his ministry was found in the gentle strength of his wife, Susannah. Their marriage faced seasons of deep strain. When Susannah became seriously ill in her thirties, she spent long stretches confined to their home. Charles, burdened with the weight of an enormous ministry, often returned exhausted, carrying frustrations from the day.

During one particularly difficult season, Charles felt overwhelmed by pressure from critics and responsibilities. His frustration sometimes crept into their conversations in ways he later regretted. Susannah, weakened by illness yet strong in spirit, responded with kindness rather than irritation. One evening, seeing worry etched across his face, she reached for his hand and said softly, "You carry more than one man should. Let me share what I can."

Her gentleness softened him instantly. He later wrote that her kindness was "a balm to my weary soul." Instead of allowing frustration to widen the distance between them, Susannah's kindness became the bridge that drew them back together.

Their marriage shows that frustration does not have to lead to conflict. Kindness, offered intentionally, turns tension into tenderness.

***

Frustration enters every marriage. It may come from exhaustion, daily pressures, misunderstandings, or unexpected challenges. When frustration rises, reactions tend to grow sharp. Tone changes. Words come quickly. Hearts close slightly. These moments can shape the emotional climate of a relationship.

Ephesians 4:32 gives a gentle but powerful instruction: "Be kind to one another, tenderhearted, forgiving one another, as God in Christ forgave you." Kindness is not weakness. It is the deliberate strength of choosing gentleness when irritation wants to speak first.

Kindness calms rising emotions. It slows down reactive patterns. It turns potential conflict into understanding. When one spouse responds with soft words or patient listening, frustration loses its power to divide.

Kindness does not ignore the problem. It simply protects the relationship while addressing it.

***

Choosing kindness when frustration rises is one of the most transformative habits in marriage. Frustration often begins small, with misunderstandings, unmet expectations, or tired evenings. Without intention, it can grow into sharp tones, emotional distance, or unnecessary conflict. Kindness interrupts this pattern. It brings calm into moments that would otherwise become heated.

Kindness begins with self awareness. Recognizing frustration early allows spouses to pause before reacting. This pause gives the heart a chance to settle and the mind a moment to think. It prevents thoughtless words from creating lasting wounds.

Another part of kindness is gentleness. A gentle tone can soften even a tense moment. When one spouse approaches the other with tenderness rather than irritation, it shifts the emotional atmosphere. Kindness communicates value, reminding both partners that the relationship matters more than the frustration.

Listening is also an expression of kindness. Sometimes frustration comes from feeling misunderstood. When spouses listen fully, without interrupting or defending, emotions begin to settle. Listening turns conflict into connection.

Forgiveness plays a role too. Kindness chooses not to escalate. It chooses to release small missteps. Forgiveness keeps irritation from turning into resentment. It makes space for understanding rather than assumption.

Practical kindness matters as well. Small acts such as taking over a task, offering a warm touch, or speaking a quiet encouragement help reset the tone of a difficult moment. These gestures communicate support even when emotions feel strained.

Kindness reflects the heart of God. Scripture consistently shows Him slow to anger and rich in compassion. When couples model this within their home, they invite peace into their marriage.

Choosing kindness during frustration does not deny emotion. It directs emotion toward unity instead of division. Over time, kindness creates a marriage where both spouses feel safe, valued, and deeply loved, even on difficult days.

FROM HIS PERSPECTIVE

I know frustration rises quickly in me when I feel overwhelmed or when expectations do not unfold the way I hoped. In those moments, my tone can shift without me noticing. What I appreciate most is when Emeline responds with kindness rather than matching my frustration. When she speaks gently, it helps me recognize my own tension. It gives me space to breathe. Her kindness calms something inside me, making it easier to talk instead of react.

I have learned that kindness is not passive. It takes strength. When I choose kindness in return, the entire moment softens. There have been evenings when she felt stretched thin, and a simple kind response from me changed the tone of our conversation. Kindness helps us understand each other instead of blaming each other. It brings us back to remembering we are a team, not opponents.

FROM HER PERSPECTIVE

Frustration can cloud my thoughts quickly when I feel tired or unprepared. In those moments, I can speak too quickly or withdraw without explaining why. What changes everything is when Emmett offers kindness instead of taking my reaction personally. When he says, "It is all right, take your time," or simply reaches for my hand, the frustration inside me loosens. I feel seen instead of judged.

I have also learned that offering kindness to him during his frustrated moments changes the atmosphere instantly. He relaxes. His shoulders drop. He begins to talk rather than shut down. Kindness makes communication safe again.

Kindness is not about ignoring frustration. It is about choosing gentleness so we can find each other through it.

PRAYER

Lord, teach us to respond with kindness when frustration rises. Help us slow our reactions, soften our tone, and offer grace instead of irritation. Fill our home with gentleness, understanding, and patience. When our emotions feel strained, remind us to turn toward one another rather than away. Give us hearts that reflect Your compassion so our marriage becomes a place of calm, unity, and steadfast love. Amen.

CONVERSATION PROMPTS

1. What situations or moments tend to trigger frustration for you most easily, and how can I respond with greater kindness during those times? Are there specific tones, gestures, or approaches that help you feel calmer and more understood when tension begins to rise?

2. When I am frustrated, what kind of kindness from you helps me settle emotionally? How can we support each other with gentleness so that frustrations become moments of connection rather than disconnection?

CONNECTION PRACTICES

Choose one moment this week to practice intentional kindness when frustration begins to rise. Offer a soft response, a calm tone, or a gentle touch. Later, talk about how that choice changed the direction of the moment. End the day by naming one act of kindness you appreciated from your spouse.

49. Extending Patience When Emotions Run High

"Wherefore, my beloved brethren, let every man
be swift to hear, slow to speak, slow to wrath."
James 1:19

It happened on a school morning that had already begun too tightly. Emeline was trying to pack lunches while searching for a missing permission slip. Emmet was helping Paldy untangle her hair, and Paldy was moving between determination and frustration with every brush stroke. She was thirteen now, old enough to want independence but still young enough to feel overwhelmed quickly.

When she finally looked in the mirror and saw a strand sticking out, her face crumpled. "It is not working," she said, and the tears came fast. Emmet paused, unsure whether to encourage or step back. Emeline stepped into the hallway just as Paldy shut her bedroom door a little too firmly.

The house grew quiet for a moment. Emeline looked at Emmet, and he gave a gentle nod. They both knew this was not about hair. It was about a heart full of middle school pressures, tiredness, and the feeling of being stretched thin.

Emeline knocked softly. "Paldy," she whispered, "we are here. Take a breath. It is all right." When the door finally opened, Paldy leaned into her mother's arms, the frustration melting with each slow breath.

That morning did not go perfectly, but patience turned a small storm into a moment of closeness.

***

Emotions rise quickly in marriage, just as they do in parenting. Stress, fatigue, pressure, or misunderstandings can make reactions sharper than intended. In those moments, patience becomes one of the most powerful gifts spouses can offer each other.

James 1:19 gives simple wisdom that fits these moments beautifully: "Let every person be quick to hear, slow to speak, slow to anger." Patience slows the rush of emotion. It gives room for perspective. It creates safety in moments that could become hurtful.

Patience does not mean ignoring feelings. It means creating space to process them without harm. When couples choose to slow down, breathe, and listen, emotional storms quiet more quickly. Hearts feel safer. Connection deepens.

Patience allows both spouses to express themselves fully while protecting the tenderness of the relationship.

***

Extending patience when emotions run high is one of the most important practices in a healthy marriage. Emotional reactions can appear suddenly. They arrive during stressful seasons, busy days, or moments of misunderstanding. Without patience, one emotional spark can ignite unnecessary conflict. With patience, couples learn to navigate feelings with gentleness and calm.

Patience begins with self control. When emotions rise, the natural impulse is to respond quickly. Patience interrupts that impulse. It allows a thoughtful breath. It gives space for a calmer response. This simple pause often prevents words that might cause regret.

Listening is another key part of patience. When one spouse feels overwhelmed or frustrated, they need to feel heard before anything else. Patient listening communicates respect and care. It allows the deeper emotion beneath the reaction to surface. When couples listen with patience, understanding grows.

Patience also involves empathy. High emotions almost always come from deeper needs: exhaustion, fear, insecurity, stress, or disappointment. When spouses look beyond the reaction to see the heart behind it, compassion increases. Emotional intensity becomes less threatening and more understandable.

Boundaries are important too. Patience does not mean allowing harmful patterns, but it does mean offering calm during temporary emotional moments. Boundaries held with gentleness protect the relationship while still honoring each person.

Patience is strengthened by prayer. Asking God for calm hearts, gentle words, and steady emotions brings peace that human willpower cannot produce. Couples who pray together in these moments create a spiritual foundation that steady emotions cannot shake.

Finally, patience creates trust. When both spouses know they can express real emotions without being met with judgment or anger, they feel safe. That safety deepens intimacy and strengthens unity.

Practicing patience in emotional moments builds a marriage where tenderness replaces tension, and grace becomes the natural response.

***

FROM HIS PERSPECTIVE

When emotions rise in our home, especially during stressful days, I sometimes feel my own tension build before I realize it. I want to fix things quickly or solve problems fast, which can make me react without thinking. But I have learned that when she or the kids are emotional, what they need most is patience, not solutions.

There was a moment recently when Emeline came home carrying more weight than she said. Her tone was shorter than usual, and for a second I felt myself getting defensive. But I paused long enough to ask, "Are you all right" Her eyes softened immediately. That simple patience opened the door for her to share what she had been holding inside.

When she extends patience toward me, it feels like a relief. It gives me room to sort my emotions without judgment. Patience turns a difficult moment into a peaceful one. It helps me feel safe, understood, and deeply cared for.

FROM HER PERSPECTIVE

When emotions rise in me, I often feel overwhelmed before I can fully explain why.

Sometimes it is stress. Sometimes it is worry. Sometimes it is simply exhaustion. What steadies me most is when Emmett slows down and offers patience instead of reacting to the emotion itself. When he listens, waits, or speaks gently, I feel seen rather than criticized.

One evening, after a long week, I found myself close to tears without knowing exactly why. He sat beside me and said quietly, "You do not have to talk yet. I am here." That patience loosened something inside me. It helped me breathe. It helped me share honestly when I was ready.

I am learning to offer him the same grace. When he feels overwhelmed or discouraged, my patience speaks more loudly than any advice could. It tells him he is safe with me. It protects our connection even when emotions feel big.

Patience changes the emotional atmosphere of our home. It keeps us close even when life feels heavy.

PRAYER

Lord, teach us to extend patience when emotions rise. Help us slow our responses, listen with compassion, and speak with gentleness. Calm the frustrations that build quickly and fill our home with Your peace. Give us wisdom to understand each other's hearts, not just reactions. Strengthen our bond through steady patience so we remain united in every season. Amen.

CONVERSATION PROMPTS

1. When your emotions feel high, what kind of patience helps you feel understood and supported instead of overwhelmed or defensive? Are there specific phrases, tones, or gestures that help you calm down more easily?

2. What makes it difficult for you to stay patient when emotions are intense, either your own or mine? How can we gently support one another in those moments so that tension does not turn into conflict?

CONNECTION PRACTICES

This week, when emotions rise, choose one intentional act of patience: slowing your tone, waiting before responding, or offering a gentle touch. Later, talk about how this changed the direction of the moment. End by expressing one thing you appreciated about your spouse's patience.

50. Holding Steady When Life Feels Uncertain

He shall not be afraid of evil tidings:
his heart is fixed, trusting in the Lord.
Psalm 112:7

In the mid twentieth century, Dr. Helen Taussig became known worldwide as a pioneering cardiologist who helped create the first successful surgery for children born with blue baby syndrome. What few people know is how much quiet strength her marriage required during the years leading up to her breakthrough work. Her demanding research hours, the emotional weight of treating fragile infants, and the burden of constant setbacks placed enormous pressure on her and on her husband, Ernest.

There was a season when Helen felt overwhelmed by uncertainty. Every experiment seemed to reach a dead end. Funding grew uncertain. Her health wavered from exhaustion. Ernest, who admired her brilliance, also carried fears he rarely admitted aloud. One evening, returning home after a failed clinical trial, Helen collapsed into a chair and whispered, "I do not know if I can continue." It was the closest she had come to giving voice to her doubts.

Ernest knelt beside her, took her hands gently, and said, "Then we will face the uncertainty together." His steadiness did not fix the problem, but it strengthened her resolve. She later wrote that his quiet faith in her was the anchor that kept her from giving up.

Their story reminds us that uncertainty does not have to divide a marriage. It can draw two hearts closer when steadiness is shared.

***

Uncertainty arrives in every marriage. It may come through finances, health concerns, unexpected news, job changes, or shifting seasons. When life feels unstable, fear can rise quickly. But Scripture gives a calming vision for hearts anchored in God.

Psalm 112:7 says, "He will have no fear of bad news; his heart is steadfast, trusting in the Lord." This verse does not promise a life without difficulty. It points to the steady inner posture of someone who trusts God even when the future feels unclear.

In marriage, holding steady together means leaning on God's faithfulness rather than depending solely on circumstances. It also means showing one another calm, compassion, and patience. When one spouse feels shaken, the other can offer steadiness through gentle words, practical help, or spiritual encouragement.

Holding steady is not pretending everything is fine. It is choosing not to face uncertainty alone.

***

Holding steady when life feels uncertain is one of the most important strengths a couple can develop. Uncertainty can unsettle the heart, cloud decisions, and create emotional tension. When fear rises, couples may withdraw, misunderstand each other, or respond with impatience. But when they choose steadiness, uncertainty becomes a moment of unity rather than division.

Steadiness begins with emotional presence. When one spouse feels overwhelmed by unknowns, the other's calm presence provides reassurance. This presence communicates, "You are not carrying this alone." Even small gestures such as sitting together, offering a gentle touch, or speaking softly can restore peace.

Steadiness also involves shared perspective. Couples strengthen each other by reminding one another of God's faithfulness, past victories, and promises from Scripture. When both spouses anchor their fears in truth rather than assumption, clarity returns.

Communication is another vital part of holding steady. Uncertainty often brings racing thoughts or unspoken worries. Honest conversations reduce anxiety and protect the relationship from unnecessary tension. Speaking and listening without fear of dismissal builds trust.

Practical action matters as well. Sometimes steadiness is expressed through taking on extra responsibilities, organizing next steps together, or helping each other create calm routines. These actions show commitment and bring structure to uncertain seasons.

Patience is an essential ingredient. Life's unknowns rarely resolve quickly. Couples who choose patience avoid frustration that could otherwise lead to conflict. They offer grace rather than pressure.

Shared prayer strengthens everything. When couples bring uncertainty before God, they exchange fear for peace. Prayer reminds them that God sees what they cannot, understands what they do not, and holds what feels unstable.

Holding steady together creates resilience. It transforms fear into partnership and unknowns into opportunities for deeper intimacy. A marriage that stands firm in uncertainty becomes a place of security, hope, and shared courage.

FROM HIS PERSPECTIVE

Uncertainty tests me in ways few other things do. When life shifts suddenly or the future feels unclear, I find myself unsettled inside. I start thinking through outcomes, trying to plan every possibility. That is usually when Emeline notices my silence or the tension in my shoulders. What helps me most is her calm presence. When she sits beside me or speaks gently, it reminds me that I do not have to carry fear by myself. Her steadiness becomes a kind of shelter.

I am learning to offer her the same steadiness. When uncertainty unsettles her, she does not always say it directly. I see it in her quietness or the way she holds her breath slightly longer than normal. When I pull her close, pray with her, or remind her that we will face this together, I feel her shoulders relax. We cannot control the future, but we can steady each other while we wait for clarity.

FROM HER PERSPECTIVE

Uncertainty affects me deeply. My thoughts start turning quickly, and I feel the weight of every possible outcome. What steadies me most is when Emmett stays near with calmness. He does not have to solve everything. His presence alone keeps my fears from growing. When he gently says, “We will walk through this together,” something inside me relaxes. I feel grounded again.

I am learning to offer him the same comfort. He carries so much that he does not always name. When I speak quietly, pray with him, or simply sit close, I see the tension leave his face. He begins to breathe more easily. Steadiness is not loud. It is a quiet strength that tells both of us we will be all right.

Uncertainty still comes, but it no longer separates us. It draws us closer.

PRAYER

Lord, when life feels uncertain, help us hold steady together. Calm our fears and remind us of Your faithfulness. Strengthen our hearts so we face the unknown with unity and trust. Teach us to offer each other gentle presence, patient love, and steady encouragement. Fill our home with peace that goes beyond circumstances. Guide our steps and keep us anchored in You through every season of uncertainty. Amen.

CONVERSATION PROMPTS

1. When life feels uncertain, what kind of support helps you feel steady rather than overwhelmed? Are there specific actions, words, or habits that bring you comfort or clarity when fear begins to rise? I want to understand how to be a calm presence for you in those moments.

2. What uncertainties in your life feel the most unsettling right now, and how can we approach them as a team? Are there rhythms or conversations that help you feel grounded while we wait for clarity?

CONNECTION PRACTICES

Choose one uncertain area in your life this week and face it together. Share your concerns, pray briefly, and decide on one small step you can take as a team. At the end of the day, reflect on how standing together affected your emotions. End with one affirmation of trust for the future.

51. Healing Old Wounds with Gentle Honesty

He healeth the broken in heart, and bindeth up their wounds.
Psalm 147:3

Marcus and Hannah had been rebuilding their marriage slowly, step by step. A few months earlier, they had reached a painful point where distractions and emotional distance nearly unraveled the bond they once treasured. Since then, they had been working intentionally to restore connection. Some days felt hopeful. Other days reminded them how fragile healing could be.

One evening, while sorting boxes in their attic, Marcus found an old journal tucked between blankets. He recognized it immediately. It belonged to Hannah, written during the season when she had felt unseen and unheard. He hesitated. His instinct was to put it back, but instead he walked downstairs and placed it gently in her hands.

She looked at the cover and froze. Marcus sat beside her quietly. "I do not want to pry," he said softly, "but I also do not want to pretend the past does not matter." Hannah opened the journal slowly, tears filling her eyes as she read words she had written in loneliness. For a moment, the old ache returned.

Marcus took her hand. "I am here now," he whispered. "And I want to understand what hurt you so deeply."

That night, they talked with a tenderness neither had expected. Gentle honesty opened a door healing had been waiting for.

***

Old wounds do not disappear simply because time has passed. They linger quietly beneath the surface, influencing reactions, emotions, and communication. Bringing these wounds into the light feels fragile, yet it is necessary for deep healing. Scripture gives comfort in moments like these.

Psalm 147:3 says, "He heals the brokenhearted and binds up their wounds." God meets us in the hidden, hurting places we often avoid. His healing is gentle and steady. He does not rush the process or ignore the pain. He restores by tending to what feels too tender to touch.

In marriage, gentle honesty reflects this same heart. It invites truth without harshness, vulnerability without fear, and reflection without accusation. When couples speak honestly about past hurt with tenderness, the wound loses its power to divide. Healing becomes possible.

Old wounds heal best when handled with compassion, patience, and a shared trust in God's restoring presence.

***

Healing old wounds with gentle honesty is essential for long term emotional closeness in marriage. Every relationship carries experiences that have shaped each spouse, including moments of hurt that may have never been fully addressed. These wounds can influence reactions, expectations, and communication patterns. Healing comes when couples courageously yet gently open space for truth, compassion, and understanding.

Gentle honesty begins with safety. Old wounds cannot be explored in the midst of defensiveness or anger. They heal when both spouses approach the conversation with patience and humility. Safety allows vulnerability. It allows tears, pauses, and moments of reflection. It invites honesty without fear of rejection.

Listening plays a central role in this process. Listening gently means receiving your spouse's story without minimizing it or rushing to defend yourself. It means honoring their experience, even when it is difficult to hear. True listening communicates respect and creates space for healing to begin.

Gentle honesty also includes owning mistakes. Apologies spoken with sincerity rebuild trust. Acknowledging past pain does not weaken the relationship. It strengthens it by removing barriers that silence and avoidance have built over time.

Compassion softens the process. Compassion sees the heart behind the hurt. It recognizes that wounds are often tied to deeper fears or unmet needs. When spouses respond with compassion, healing unfolds more naturally.

Patience is important as well. Old wounds rarely heal in one conversation. They heal through repeated moments of tenderness, steady reassurance, and continued understanding. Couples who remain patient with each other's emotional pace build a foundation of lasting unity.

Prayer strengthens the process. Inviting God into the wounded places allows His peace to steady the heart and His truth to guide the conversation. Healing becomes a shared journey rather than a burden carried alone.

When couples choose gentle honesty, old wounds lose their ability to fracture connection. Marriage becomes a place of restoration, tenderness, and renewed trust.

FROM HIS PERSPECTIVE

There are wounds I have carried for years, some I barely understood myself. When they get touched accidentally, my reactions come out sharper or quieter than I intend. What has helped me most is my wife's gentle honesty. She does not pry, but she also does not ignore the moments she sees pain rising in me. When she asks softly, "Can you tell me what you are feeling," I feel my defenses lower. Her voice gives me permission to speak without fear of being misunderstood.

I am learning to offer the same gentleness to her. When she shares past hurt, I want to listen carefully rather than rushing to fix it. I want to understand the deeper parts of her heart. Gentle honesty has shown me that healing does not come from solutions. It comes from presence. It comes from compassion. It comes from the quiet promise that we will walk through these wounds together until peace replaces pain.

FROM HER PERSPECTIVE

Old wounds have a way of resurfacing when life becomes stressful. Sometimes I do not expect them. A phrase, a tone, or a moment can bring back emotions I thought I had already sorted through. What helps me heal is when he approaches those moments with tenderness rather than frustration. When Emmett says gently, "I really do want to understand," I feel safe enough to share what hurts.

I am learning to offer him the same patience. He carries wounds he rarely talks about, and when he opens up, I see how deeply he needs compassion instead of correction. Gentle honesty allows both of us to share without shame. It turns emotional pain into a moment of closeness rather than conflict.

Healing old wounds requires courage, but it also requires kindness. When we slow down, listen carefully, and choose tenderness, healing becomes possible. We find connection in places that were once painful.

PRAYER

Lord, heal the hidden wounds we still carry. Give us courage to speak honestly and gently. Help us listen with compassion, respond with tenderness, and create safety for vulnerable conversations. Bind up the places where pain has lingered and restore peace where fear once settled. Fill our marriage with Your healing presence so that old wounds lose their power and new closeness grows in their place. Amen.

CONVERSATION PROMPTS

1. Are there old wounds that still influence how you feel or react, even if they seem small? How can I approach those tender places with gentleness and understanding so you feel safe rather than guarded or pressured?

2. When you share past hurt, what responses from me help you feel heard and supported? Are there ways I can offer more compassion or patience so healing comes more easily?

CONNECTION PRACTICES

Choose one old memory or lingering hurt to discuss gently this week. Approach the conversation with softness, patience, and curiosity. Afterward, affirm one strength you see in your spouse that has grown from past pain. End with a brief prayer for healing together.

52. Choosing Commitment Every Single Day

Intreat me not to leave thee, or to return from following after thee:
for whither thou goest, I will go; and where thou lodgest, I will lodge:
thy people shall be my people, and thy God my God:
Where thou diest, will I die, and there will I be buried:
the Lord do so to me, and more also, if ought but death part thee and me.
Ruth 1:16–17

The road stretched long before them as dust rose around their sandals. Naomi walked slowly, her grief still fresh, her future uncertain. Ruth walked beside her with quiet determination. Everything familiar to Ruth lay behind her. Her homeland. Her culture. Her family. Yet she stayed close to Naomi, matching her steps, supporting her through the weight of loss.

There was a moment when Naomi paused on the road. She looked at Ruth with weary eyes and said, "Return to your people. You do not have to bear this with me." Naomi wanted to release her from responsibility, believing Ruth deserved a life unburdened by her sorrow.

Ruth did not waver. She stepped closer and spoke words that have echoed for generations: "Where you go, I will go, and where you stay, I will stay. Your people shall be my people, and your God my God." Her voice held no hesitation. Her commitment was not based on convenience or ease. It was a deliberate choice shaped by love, loyalty, and faith.

They continued walking together until they reached Bethlehem, where their story would unfold into redemption neither of them could have imagined. Their journey began not with certainty, but with daily, steady commitment.

***

Ruth's declaration to Naomi is one of Scripture's clearest expressions of unwavering commitment. Her promise was not built on emotion or ideal circumstances. It was made in the middle of loss, instability, and unknown futures. Ruth teaches that commitment is not a feeling. It is a daily decision.

In marriage, commitment deepens when couples choose one another intentionally, especially in seasons that challenge comfort. Ruth 1:16–17 shows how commitment strengthens relationship. It creates safety, steadiness, and direction. It says, "You will not walk alone," even when life changes suddenly.

Commitment in marriage is strengthened through presence, faithfulness, and shared trust in God. It means staying connected through difficulty, choosing unity during uncertainty, and remembering the vows that were spoken with sincerity. Commitment creates a foundation where love grows deeper every day.

***

Choosing commitment every single day is the heart of a lasting marriage. Commitment does not erase hardship or prevent conflict, but it provides the stability needed to face both with courage. A committed marriage is not shaped by perfection, but by two people who keep choosing one another even when circumstances feel heavy.

Commitment begins with intention. Every day offers small opportunities to reaffirm love through words, actions, and presence. Speaking gently, listening thoughtfully, and giving consistent affection communicate, "I am here, and I am choosing you." These small acts build emotional security.

Another part of commitment is perseverance. Seasons of difficulty such as financial strain, health challenges, misunderstandings, or external pressures can test a marriage. Commitment steadies the heart through those times. It shifts the focus from temporary discomfort to long term unity.

Commitment also requires forgiveness. No marriage can thrive without it. Forgiveness removes the barriers that mistakes create. It clears space for healing, reconnection, and renewed trust.

Shared purpose strengthens commitment. Couples who grow spiritually together, set goals together, and support each other's dreams strengthen the bond that holds them through uncertainty. Shared purpose reminds them they are building a life, not just surviving moments.

Another essential part is daily presence. Commitment grows through showing up emotionally, not merely physically. Presence reminds each spouse that they are valued, respected, and loved intentionally.

Finally, spiritual grounding deepens commitment. When a marriage is rooted in God's wisdom and sustained through prayer, the relationship gains an unshakable foundation. God's presence provides the strength, compassion, and resilience needed to love faithfully through every season.

Commitment is not a one time promise. It is a daily choice that builds a marriage capable of enduring, healing, and flourishing.

***

FROM HIS PERSPECTIVE

There are days when commitment feels easy and days when it feels like a deliberate decision. I have learned that choosing commitment daily creates strength I did not know I needed. Commitment means showing up even when I am tired, listening even when I feel distracted, and standing close even when emotions feel complicated. When I choose Emeline, consistently and intentionally, our marriage grows steadier. I see how much it matters to her when I stay emotionally present and faithful in the small moments. That steadiness becomes a shield for both of us.

There are also days when I need her commitment in ways I cannot always explain. When she stays beside me, encourages me, or reminds me gently that we are still in this together, my confidence rises. Her commitment strengthens me, especially when I am uncertain. It reminds me that we are building something enduring, something worth protecting every day.

FROM HER PERSPECTIVE

Commitment is something I feel deeply, not just in my thoughts but in my actions. There are days when loving Emmett comes naturally and days when I have to lean into grace and choose love intentionally. When I choose commitment, I see how it steadies us both. It helps me stay close even when emotions shift or when life feels overwhelming. Commitment reminds me that small choices build a strong foundation.

When he shows his commitment, I feel secure. I feel valued. I feel protected. His consistency gives me confidence. Even in difficult conversations or stressful seasons, his willingness to stay engaged communicates love more loudly than any words. Commitment gives us room to grow, to heal, and to understand each other more deeply. It turns challenges into opportunities to strengthen our bond.

PRAYER

Lord, help us choose commitment every single day. Strengthen our hearts with faithfulness, patience, and unity. Teach us to show love through small actions, gentle words, and steady presence. Remind us of the vows we made and the grace You give to keep them. Fill our home with perseverance when life feels heavy and with joy when days are light. Keep us anchored in Your love so our marriage grows stronger in every season. Amen.

CONVERSATION PROMPTS

1. What daily actions or gestures from me make you feel most secure in our commitment? Are there simple habits we can build that help us reaffirm our dedication to one another even on busy or difficult days?

2. Are there areas of our relationship where you need more reassurance or consistency from me? How can we strengthen our commitment by communicating more clearly, supporting more intentionally, and choosing unity more deliberately?

CONNECTION PRACTICES

This week, choose one small daily action that communicates commitment: a gentle touch, an encouraging word, a moment of presence, or an act of service. At the end of the week, share how these choices strengthened your connection. End with a prayer of gratitude for the journey you have walked together.